D1014832

BEYOND
THE
COSMOS

"In *Beyond the Cosmos*, Dr. Ross has shown that the tools scientists have used to deal with paradoxes in the physical world can also be applied to gain important insight into various paradoxes in Scripture. Difficulties that have plagued the Christian community for centuries are not only clarified when 'seen' from the point of view of one living in a higher dimension, but those same difficulties also become the basis for strong proof of the supernatural inspiration of the Bible. This book will provide food for thought for any student of the Word and will, no doubt, begin a new area of biblical research to which others can contribute."

—David Rogstad, Ph.D., physicist, Caltech Jet Propulsion Laboratory

"In *Beyond the Cosmos*, Dr. Hugh Ross considers application to theology of current scientific research suggesting that our universe may be more than four- dimensional. He suggest that we can use the general concept of extra-spatial and temporal dimensions to further our understanding of God of the nature of existence outside this universe. *Beyond the Cosmos* is a thought-provoking book, sure in inspire much discussion and contemplation."

—Dr. Gerald B. Cleaver, postdoctoral researcher in elementary particle physics, Ohio State University

"Not since the decade before the first world war has a Christian thinker given so much attention to the dimensional distinctions and boundaries that have been opened up in scientific discover of a multi-dimensional universe, and reflected on what the demands of us in biblical and evangelical faith today. Hugh Ross offers readers a fresh and illuminating approach to thinking about God and divine revelation in open-structured and extra-dimensional ways that will be a great help to many people today."

—Thomas F. Torrance, professor, The University of Edinburgh

THE EXTRA-DIMENSIONALITY OF GOD

BEYOND THE COSMOS

WHAT RECENT DISCOVERIES IN ASTRONOMY AND
PHYSICS REVEAL ABOUT THE NATURE OF GOD

HUGH ROSS, PH.D.

NAVPRESS

BRINGING TRUTH TO LIFE

NavPress Publishing Group
P.O. Box 35001, Colorado Springs, Colorado 80935

The Navigators is an international Christian organization. Our mission is to reach, disciple, and equip people to know Christ and to make Him known through successive generations. We envision multitudes of diverse people in the United States and every other nation who have a passionate love for Christ, live a lifestyle of sharing Christ's love, and multiply spiritual laborers among those without Christ.

NavPress is the publishing ministry of The Navigators. NavPress publications help believers learn biblical truth and apply what they learn to their lives and ministries. Our mission is to stimulate spiritual formation among our readers.

Library of Congress Catalog Card Number: 96-15633
ISBN 08910-99646

Cover design: David Carlson

Some of the anecdotal illustrations in this book are true to life and are included with the permission of the persons involved. All other illustrations are composites of real situations, and any resemblance to people living or dead is coincidental.

Unless otherwise identified, all Scripture quotations in this publication are taken from the HOLY BIBLE: NEW INTERNATIONAL VERSION ® (NIV®). Copyright © 1973, 1978, 1984 by International Bible Society. Used by permission of Zondervan Publishing House. All rights reserved. Other version used include the *New American Standard Bible* (NASB), © The Lockman Foundation 1960, 1962, 1963, 1968, 1971, 1972, 1973, 1975, 1977; and the *King James Version*.

Ross, Hugh (Hugh Norman), 1945-
    Beyond the cosmos : the extra-dimensionality of God : what recent discoveries in astronomy and physics reveal about the nature of God / Hugh Ross.
        p.   cm.
    Includes bibliographical references and indexes.
    ISBN 0-89109-964-6 (hardcover)
    1. God. 2. Time—Religious aspects—Christianity. 3. Astronomy—Religious aspects—Christianity. 4. Physics—Religious aspects—Christianity. I. Title.
BT102.R667   1996
261.5'5—dc20   96-15633
                                                          CIP

Printed in the United States of America

1 2 3 4 5 6 7 8 9 10 11 12 13 14 15 / 00 99 98 97 96

CONTENTS

LIST OF FIGURES AND TABLES

Figures

Tables

ACKNOWLEDGMENTS

Though my name appears on this book's cover, no room would be left for the title or anything else if it included the names of all those who contributed significantly to its development. I may be the lyricist and lead singer in this oratorio, but I have a large and gifted choir singing with me. In fact, if you listen carefully, you can hear a duet, in unison with my wife, Kathy, who blends her voice with mine throughout the piece to enhance the clarity of the lyrics.

Janet Kobobel Grant served expertly in the conductor's role, keeping the production moving and shaping it for maximum impact. Her voice can be heard, too, in the many trio passages. Janet's assistants included George Bell, Bonnie Connoley, Miguel Endara, Joyce Magee, and Sherry Russell.

A team of consultants and coaches took time out from their own scholarly pursuits to offer substantial suggestions for improving the original work: Gerald Cleaver, Sam Conner, Craig Keener, Alex Metherell, John Rea, and Mick Ukleja. Marj Harman and Mal Scharer served as my research assistants.

The Paradoxes Sunday school class at Sierra Madre Congregational Church provided the rehearsal hall—and audience—during the composition process. These folks offered encouragement, prayer, and invaluable feedback.

Sheila Cherney, Lucille Dennis, Tadd Sutton, and the rest of my office staff did everything in their power to streamline my executive duties for several months so that I would have time to write. All participated in critiquing and revising the final draft.

Also working hard and inconspicuously behind the scenes were the many family members and friends who took care of our children, our pets, our home, and even our car repairs when the writing and editing became most intense. Special thanks to Patty Bradbury, Mara and Mark Clark, Elaina and Gary Drake, Myrtle and Ward Drake, Kay and Ken Hoevel, Carol and Eric Notti, Debbie and Russ Pershing, and Zana and Steve Scheele.

The courage to attempt an integration of scientific findings with biblical revelation about extra-dimensionality arose from the wholehearted enthusiasm of NavPress Editorial Director Steve Webb and his editorial team.

Kathy and I want all of these individuals and our readers to know how grateful we are for the deepening of faith and joy we experienced day after day as we studied and wrote and rewrote. What we sought to offer Him—and you—as a gift became His gift to us.

CHAPTER ONE

AN INVITATION TO SOAR

Can we really know God, know Him in a relational sort of way? We Christians often say that spiritual life is not about religion but about a relationship with our Creator and Savior. This declaration has a nice ring to it, especially to those who recognize relationships as life's core program, not just as interesting electives.

But how successful can we be in developing a relationship with someone we cannot physically see, hear, or touch? The relationships we are most familiar with—and continually strive to learn more about through books, seminars, tapes, articles, courses, sermons, lectures, agencies, and whole industries—are the ones with fellow human beings (and even pets!). We are especially eager—some would say desperate—to fulfill our longing for intimate, lasting relationships that allow us to know and be known, accept and be accepted, cherish and be cherished, all with a depth and breadth that grows through time.

If God is a personal Being, as the Bible says, what we have learned from human relationships should allow us to make some applications to building a relationship with Him. And what could be more desirable than an experiential connection with unlimited Love, Life, and Truth? We want it; so does He, according to the Bible. We follow through on the commitment He asks of us and the journey begins. We learn very soon why He promises to be faithful when we are faithless.[1] We learn to say to the Lord, "I do believe; help me overcome my unbelief!"[2] We are glad for the encouragement of others who embarked on this relationship before we did. We look to them for reassurance.

Several distinguished theologians have offered able assistance. They have focused our attention on God's character qualities and divine attributes, exhorting us to fix our minds on these things. They have reminded us to talk with Him, to acknowledge His presence in and around us daily, moment by moment. They have given us practical instruction in worship. I value the work of these godly men and women, and I have seen its positive impact in my own and others' lives. And yet we still have much room to grow.

Because we cannot use our five senses (as we do with people) to detect God's presence, His voice, or the feelings and attitudes behind His words, we often struggle with doubts and misgivings. We cannot picture Him, at least not in His totality. And so many of His characteristics and doctrines seem contradictory that we do not know how to hold Him in our mind's eye. Even when we invent pictures and ways to visualize Him, we are cautiously aware of the dangers of distortion.

If we are anything like the people portrayed in the Bible, we wish "God with us" were much more tangible. Which of us does not sometimes question, as the first disciples did, why it is better for us if Christ (our physical proof of God's reality, power, and love) returns to heaven and sends the invisible Comforter, Counselor, Holy Spirit in His stead? Since Jesus said it, we accept it. Nonetheless, we wrestle with it. If only we could get a better grip on *how* it is better!

I believe God has just enabled us to tighten our grip. He has proven, again, His willingness to disclose Himself for the sake of strengthening and deepening our relationship with Him and of drawing others to join us in that venture. In the pages that follow, I will describe a remarkable set of scientific discoveries made in the mid-1990s that may open our understanding to some of the greatest mysteries of the ages such as:

✦ How can my choices be totally "free" if God is in control of all things at all times, if He knows the end from the beginning?

✦ How can He hear my words and thoughts while listening to billions of others around the world at exactly the same moment?

✦ How can God be forever alive and still suffer death (in the person of Christ) on the cross?

✦ How can God be all-powerful and all-loving and yet allow so much suffering and evil?

✦ How can God be both three *and* one?

These "how can it be?" mysteries have for centuries tested the faith and love of those who believe in the biblical, personal God, and often have served as stumbling blocks for those who do not.

The test presented to Christians by these mysteries has been for us to honor Him as the Truth, whose name is also Teacher, and to respect each other as students. We know our assignment is to study, dialogue, and discern, but instead we often dispute and divide. I hope we will use these breakthrough discoveries to help us resolve our differences.

These discoveries offer new insights into God's mind-boggling capacities in His mind-boggling eleven (the newly proven *minimum*) dimensions of reality. Whatever mental pictures we hold of Him will have to be expanded enormously. Though never complete in this life, they will be more complete than before. We will know how God can be nearer to us than our own breath, nearer even than the person with whom we are most intimate. We will understand why it is better for Jesus to be where He is than to remain physically present with us. We will gain a clearer picture of where He is now and what heaven will be like. Comprehension of these capacities can launch us into greater heights of rejoicing and new depths of appreciation, individually and collectively, for the immeasurable gift of eternity with Him.

For those who have not yet begun such a relationship, I hope that an exploration of these capacities will inspire not only awe but also a vision and desire for the possibilities of such a relationship.

Let's soar together through these newly charted regions beyond the matter, energy, and old space-time boundaries of the cosmos.

CHAPTER TWO

TAKEOFF FROM GROUND ZERO

We are about to explore the wonder and glory of God in eleven (at least) dimensions of space and time. But before we burst through the current space-time manifold of the universe for a glimpse at God's extra-dimensional realm, let's discuss what dimensionality is all about. (Readers with little scientific and math training may find that chapters 2 and 3 require more concentration. Other chapters are readily accessible to all readers.)

Most people never think about dimensions, except in geometry and architecture classes, for the simple reason that our dimensional realm never changes. Since birth we have lived in the four dimensions of length, width, height, and time. We will continue to reside there until the day of our physical death. The laws of physics God designed for us require that all the matter and energy of the universe be situated on (and confined to) the manifold, or "envelope," of these four dimensions.[1]

Each of the four space-time dimensions of the physical universe is independent of the others. For example, in the length dimension we can extend a line as long or as short as we like without affecting any measures in the width, height, or time dimensions. Similarly, lines can be extended as far as we desire, even infinitely far, along each of the dimensions of width, height, and time without affecting measurements in the other three dimensions. This independence means that each dimension always must be exactly perpendicular—exactly at a ninety-degree angle—to all the other dimensions (in Euclidean geometries).

We cannot picture in our minds how the time dimension intersects our three space dimensions, yet we experience the effects of time and we can measure its reality as an independent dimension. What we must keep in mind is that our capacity to visualize things will be limited to the three space dimensions that our five senses can directly detect.

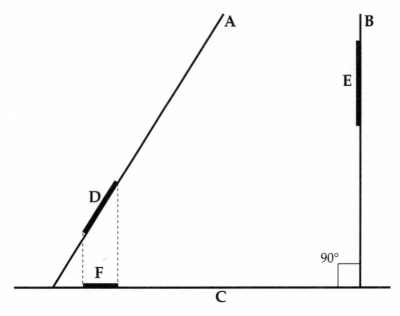

Figure 2.1: Dependent Versus Independent Dimensions
Dimension **A** is not independent from dimension **C** because a projection from dimension **A** (such as **D**) will cast a shadow (**F**) on dimension **C**. Dimension **B** is independent from dimension **C** because a projection from dimension **B** (such as **E**) will create a point rather than a shadow on dimension **C**.

The difference between a dependent and an independent dimension is shown in figure 2.1. Lines drawn along the dependent dimension (A) project (as in casting a shadow) on the alternate dimension (C). All lines drawn along the independent dimension (B) make no such projection. They will show up only as infinitesimally small points.

Adding Dimensions
A one-dimensional realm is a single line. That realm includes only points and lines fixed along that one-dimensional line. Let's call that

line "length." A two-dimensional realm is a plane. It is described by two lines that are always at right angles (90 degrees) to each other (assuming Euclidean geometry). Let's call these lines "length" and "width." In such a realm, points, lines, and two-dimensional figures—polygons, circles, ellipses, and countless other shapes residing in the plane—are possible.

A three-dimensional realm is a volume defined by three dimensions. Each line defining one of the dimensions is at right angles to both of the other two lines (see figure 2.2). Let's call these lines "length," "width," and "height." In this realm, points, lines, two-dimensional figures, and three-dimensional solids or volumes are possible.

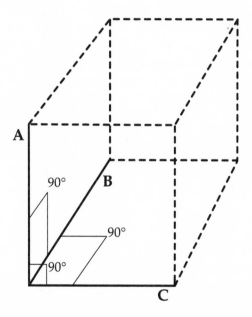

Figure 2.2: A Two-Dimensional Depiction of a Three-Dimensional Realm
This illustration of a box shows three-dimension-defining lines: **A** (height), **B** (length), and **C** (width) each at right angles to the other two, as 90 ° angle markers on the box's sides indicate.

To construct a four-dimensional realm we need four dimension-defining lines, each line lying at right angles to the other dimension-defining lines. Let's call these dimensions "length," "width," "height," and "time." Such a realm is the realm of our existence. But because we cannot place ourselves beyond the four—say, in a fifth dimension where we could gain some perspective—we cannot picture all four simultaneously. We are limited to picturing only three. This limitation struck me and my fellow students forcibly one day in a college course on complex algebra.

The professor described how in four dimensions of space, a three-dimensional basketball could be turned inside out without making any breaks in its surface. None of us could picture how. But, given the mathematics of four independent dimensions of space, we could, without too much difficulty, demonstrate that the professor was right. Such a phenomenon could indeed occur. We had proved it, but we could not visualize it, and we felt uncomfortable with that limitation.

Then our professor referred us to a film. By animating two dimensions at a time, the filmmaker actually depicted a basketball turning inside out without breaking its surface. This film frustrated us even more. We could see from different perspectives (various "top," "bottom," "side," etc., views) how the transformation progressed, yet we could not unify in our minds the various two-dimensional images into one four-dimensional picture. In the end, we were forced to let go of the frustration and be satisfied with our equations. That step was a big one, and an important one for the sake of ongoing research.

Subtracting Dimensions

Architects use the same technique the filmmaker did in showing us the basketball phenomenon. The big difference, however, is that the architects' clients are not asked to cross a dimensional threshold. A three-dimensional building is portrayed to three-space-dimension people by showing them various two-dimensional cross sections. A plan view (from above) and side views from the east, west, north, south (and possibly other angles as well) suffice to give the clients a detailed mental picture of how the building will look.

This technique works because the architects' clients live in three dimensions of space. But what if the clients were deprived of just one dimension of space? If they were confined to the length and width dimensions alone, with no visual access to the dimension of height, they would experience the same frustration in trying to visualize buildings as my class did in trying to picture a basketball turning inside out in four space dimensions.

These two-space-dimension creatures would, however, be capable of determining the properties of the three-dimensional building. Once convinced that three space dimensions are possible, they could mathematically add an extra space dimension to the two-dimensional mathematics they normally work with. Then they could establish which attributes and descriptions of the building could be true and which could not. Ultimately, they, too, would have to deal with visual limitations and accept the equations.

Beyond the Fourth Dimension

The method we algebra students used to construct mathematically a realm of four space dimensions can be used to build realms of virtually any number of dimensions. With five dimension-defining lines, each line at right angles to the other four, we can describe a five-dimensional world. With six such lines, we can mathematically describe a six-dimensional realm. And so on. For each of these n-dimensional worlds we formulate geometrically, we can design algebraic expressions to describe what shapes and functions are possible for physical entities existing in those n dimensions.

With the help of supercomputers, mathematicians have designed realms with as many as a million dimensions of space. Their n-dimensional equations can predict what phenomena are possible in each of these n-dimensional worlds. One of the patterns they observe is that the more dimensions in a realm, the closer certain odd-shaped objects, such as spheres, can be packed together.

This higher dimensional mathematics makes for a fun exercise, but does it have any practical significance if extra dimensions beyond length, width, height, and time (what mathematicians typically call D5, D6, D7, etc. or De, Df, Dg, etc.) do not exist? Not really, but the exciting news is that these mathematical exercises have prepared us to grapple with new discoveries about reality.

What physicists have discovered in the past several months can be neither understood nor appreciated without such mathematical tools. I cannot help but say the timing is perfect. Physicists have just uncovered strong evidence that extra dimensions do indeed exist.

Yet predating these physics discoveries by more than nineteen hundred years are the words of the prophets and apostles who penned the sixty-six books of the Bible. These ancients described phenomena—such as the creation event, miracles, Jesus' post-resurrection capacities, as well as paradoxical doctrines—that require the existence of extra dimensions or the functional equivalent of extra dimensions. The writers assured their readers that God's ways and thoughts are beyond our human limits, that "eternity," some unknown reality beyond this universe, is somehow inscribed within us.

Now we have the opportunity and the privilege to see from a new perspective—and to integrate—what yesterday's Bible authors and today's physicists affirm about reality beyond the cosmos.

CHAPTER THREE

SCIENCE BREAKS THROUGH TO NEW REALMS

The first hint at the existence of extra dimensions (dimensions beyond length, width, height, and time) came via Einstein's theory of general relativity. Almost at a glance, the set of ten general relativity equations indicates an ultimate origin for matter and energy. Even without the detailed calculations, a picture emerges from those equations, a picture of simultaneous expansion and deceleration. Only one phenomenon in physics fits this picture: an explosion. A closer study of these general relativity equations reveals that the entire universe burst forth and is still expanding outward from an infinitely (or nearly infinitely) dense state.[1]

This creation event, often called the Big Bang, has been confirmed in several ways through the past few decades of research.[2] The most direct evidence comes from measurements of the distances and motions of the galaxies[3-4] and of the temperature and characteristics of the initial explosion's radiation residue at varying distances from us.[5-9] This bursting forth of the cosmos from an infinitely small volume, or essentially an infinitely small volume (a few cosmological models predict an initial maximum volume of 10^{-100} or 0.00000000000000000000000000000000000000000000000000000000000000 00000000000000000000000000000000000000000000001 cubic centimeters), implies that the universe has a beginning, a starting point in the finite past. Einstein recognized this implication[10] and dared to say that it affirms the necessity of "a superior reasoning power."[11]

Space-Time Theorem Emerges

Einstein's conclusion went against the grain of astronomers and physicists trained to presume an infinite universe and an irrelevant, if any, Initiator. The simplicity and obvious nature of his conclusion made it all the more irritating.[12-18] Several attempts were made to prove that this finite beginning arose from incorrect assumptions about the universe's homogeneity and symmetry.[19] Critics tried introducing all manner of inhomogeneities, asymmetries, and rotations into Einstein's theory, but to their amazement, these machinations backfired. They actually slightly shortened the time scale back to the beginning.[20] No matter how astrophysicists manipulated the theory, this stubborn singularity (the infinitesimally small volume threshold at which matter and energy began) would not go away.

It was left to the next generation of astrophysicists to figure out why it would not, could not, go away. Over a four-year period, starting in 1966, George Ellis, Stephen Hawking, and Roger Penrose affirmed that any expanding universe governed by general relativity and which also contains at least some matter and energy must possess a singular origin in the finite past.[21-24] But they went further. In fact, they carried the solution of Einstein's equations further than anyone else had. In doing so, they discovered that the operation of general relativity guarantees a singular boundary not just for matter and energy but also for space and time. In other words, if general relativity accurately describes the physics of the universe, both the stuff that makes up the universe and the dimensions in which that stuff exists and operates share a common origin, a finite beginning. We call this finding the space-time theorem of general relativity, and it carries profound significance.

In 1970, however, that crucial *if* still hung over general relativity. Expansion was no longer in doubt; the existence of matter and energy never had been in doubt. And though the operation of general relativity had been affirmed—to 1 percent precision (two decimal places)[25-27]—it had not yet been established with adequate certainty to put theoreticians' doubts to rest.[28] By 1980, the level of certainty had improved to better than a hundredth percent precision (four decimal places)[29]—impressive, and yet still not quite enough to satisfy the most skeptical.[30] But in 1993, the lingering shred of uncertainty finally flew away.

The Nobel Prize in physics that year went to Russell Hulse and Joseph Taylor for their study of the binary pulsar PSR 1913+16. This stellar system is unique: two neutron stars (one of which is also a pulsar) orbit closely about one another. Through a twenty-year-long study of this system—in which gravitational forces exceed those seen in our solar system by hundreds of thousands of times—a team lead by Taylor was able to affirm the accuracy of general relativity to better than a trillionth percent precision (that is, to fourteen decimal places).[31-32] In Penrose's words, this set of measurements "makes Einstein's general relativity, in this particular sense, the most accurately tested theory known to science!"[33]

Second Dimension of Time

The space-time theorem is no longer in question. Nor is its corollary that the cause (Causer) of the universe operates in a dimension of time or its equivalent (that is, maintains some attribute, capacity, super-dimensionality, or supra-dimensionality that permits the equivalent of cause and effect operations) completely independent of ours. The law of causality (or the law of statistical correlation in which quantum or statistical mechanical effects are significant) says that effects emanate from causes and not the other way around. Thus, causes precede their effects. Time, then, can be defined as a dimension along which cause and effect phenomena occur.

The creation event—the origin of the universe's matter, energy, and dimensionality—is an effect that includes our time dimension. Whoever caused the universe, then, must possess at least one more time dimension (or some attribute, capacity, super-dimension, or supra-dimension that encompasses all the properties of time). To put it another way, God is able to interact with us in ways we interpret (through our time-bound experience of cause and effect) as the result of timelike capacities in the person or essence of God or the existence of other timelike dimensions through which God operates.

In this space-time theorem and its corollary, we find confirmation of the biblical revelation of a Creator who exists and operates beyond our time dimension and who is in no way confined to it. In other words, the Creator's capacities include at least two, perhaps more, time dimensions. Just imagine for a moment what His time capacities, cause and effect capacities, must be. No wonder He calls Himself the "I AM," the Alpha and the Omega. (We'll delve into the deeper theological implications of God's time dimensionality in later chapters.)

Unified Field Theories

Still more breakthroughs have come and are coming. Physicists can now demonstrate that the Causer exists and operates in several spatial dimensions beyond our three, as well as in at least one more time dimension (or the equivalent).

This rapidly unfolding drama started more than a half century ago in the quest for a single elegant theory that would explain the relationship of all four forces of physics, a "unified field theory." Einstein devoted the last twenty-five years of his life to this ambitious quest. He failed to achieve his goal, not for lack of brilliance, but for lack of technological tools: particle accelerators powerful enough to produce the extended family of fundamental particles and to probe unification energies; supercomputers capable of generating various solutions to sets of complex non-linear differential equations; ground- and space-based telescopes capable of penetrating the farthest reaches of the cosmos to its earliest moments of existence. (The more distant a galaxy, the longer it took that light to reach us and therefore the farther back in time we are peering.)

Einstein did succeed in his goal in one significant sense: He paved the way to development of that magnificent theory. In developing special relativity, he showed how matter and energy are interchangeable under certain conditions. In general relativity, he showed how space and time, as well as matter and energy, are interchangeable under certain conditions. The key to this interchangeability, or "unification," was the addition of a dimension. When the traditional three-dimensional approach got him nowhere, Einstein proposed a four-dimensional system requiring calculations in 4-D, rather than 3-D, geometry. He treated time as a fourth dimension, virtually equivalent to length, width, and height. And his approach worked.

Einstein's addition of a dimension unifying matter and energy (special relativity) and eventually matter, energy, length, width, height, and time (general relativity), set today's generation of physicists on the right track. By adding not just one but several dimensions of space to our three, they may well have accomplished what once seemed impossible. The latest research findings demonstrate that electromagnetism, the weak and strong nuclear forces, and gravity—the four fundamental forces of physics—can be unified in a ten-dimensional realm.

The first observational indication came in the 1970s and early 1980s when newly available one-hundred-billion-electron-volt particle accelerators brought physicists success in unifying electromagnetism and the weak nuclear force into one force, the electroweak force.[34-37] Their efforts showed, at least to some extent, that force unification is possible.

A series of 1990s experiments using much more powerful particle accelerators aided in the discovery of several dozen fundamental particles, including the six quarks predicted by theories explaining the unification of the strong and weak nuclear forces with the electromagnetic force.[38-39] Based on these findings, researchers are confident that the strong nuclear force, too, must be unifiable with the electroweak force. Exactly how has yet to be observed, but particle physicists have theoretically established that such unification will occur at energy levels of about a trillion trillion electron volts (a trillion times more energy than the highest levels achieved to date in particle accelerator experiments).

Strings
The theoretical and observational success of supersymmetry convinced researchers that extra space dimensions must exist. This new perspective on reality became possible only because researchers would not give up in the face of a seemingly intractable problem. As long as they treated fundamental particles as points, all attempts at unification failed. Worse yet, their equations yielded absurd conditions for the universe at ultra high temperatures.

Something was wrong, but what? Fundamental particles look like points and behave like points, but because models treating them as points developed problems at high temperature conditions, conditions very near the beginning of the cosmos, obviously the models were incorrect. What if fundamental particles looked and behaved like something other than points in the newborn universe? Through painstaking effort scientists found that if fundamental particles function as loops of energy, what physicists call "strings," unification theories and the entire array of physics theories—even special and general relativity and quantum mechanics—may work together.

A Close-up on Strings

Strings are less like strings than they are like vibrating, rotating elastic bands. They are greatly stretched at the extremely high temperature of the first split second of the universe's existence. At the lower temperatures since then, they are contracted to such a degree (typically they are a hundred billion billion times smaller than a proton) that they behave like points.

String theories do not work in three space dimensions. They need much more room to operate. However, they need that room—six extra space dimensions—only for a moment, just a split second after the initial creative burst. From that moment on, these six extra dimensions are no longer necessary to the universe's development. So, what happened to the six?

For many months scientists grappled with literally thousands of possible answers to that question. Because of the enormous complexity of the string theory equations, more than a hundred million possible mathematical solutions existed; and, because our knowledge of conditions in the earliest moments of the universe lacks necessary precision, determining which of these solutions correctly described reality posed a daunting problem.

Math Breakthrough Solves String Problem

In the latter weeks of 1994, while people around the world prepared to celebrate Christmas, physicists Ed Witten and Nathan Seiberg gave their own special gift to humanity. They reduced an entire field of mathematics to a single short paper. For decades mathematicians were stymied in their attempts to describe with precision certain physics phenomena requiring four-dimensional space. Their equations seemed impossible to solve, even with supercomputers. But a pair of super human brains did it. Witten and Seiberg transformed these extremely complex equations into simple ones, almost as simple as the calculus equations so familiar to undergraduates.[40]

While string theorists recognized almost immediately that they had just received a boost toward success, even the optimists assumed that producing a workable theory would take at least a few more years of hard work. To their surprise and joy, the crucial breakthrough came in a matter of months.

Witten and Seiberg helped by eliminating an annoying physical absurdity from supersymmetry theory. When Witten and Seiberg introduced a hypothetical massive particle that has the potential to become massless, the absurdity vanished.[41] Taking a clue from this approach, physicist Andrew Strominger proposed a certain type of black hole, what he calls a "charged extremal black hole," as the possible solution to a similar problem encountered in string theory.[41] Strominger later teamed up with physicist Brian Greene and mathematician David Morrison to demonstrate that charged extremal black holes can transform into fundamental particles, and vice versa, in a manner similar to ice turning into liquid water and liquid water into ice.[41-42]

GALLERY OF STRINGS

Though strings are just one-dimensional line elements, they can behave in exotic ways in multiple space dimensions. Heterotic strings, for example, are closed loops with two types of vibrations. The clockwise vibration operates in ten dimensions of space, the counterclockwise in twenty-six dimensions (sixteen of which have been compactified). In a six-dimensional realm, a five-dimensional analog to the one-dimensional string appears, namely, a five-brane, a five-dimensional supermembrane. Type II strings also appear. In the dimensional realm where these strings operate, electric charges disappear. In four dimensions of space, solitons appear. These particle-like objects include magnets with only one pole (i.e., magnetic monopoles).

As an unexpected bonus, Strominger, Greene, and Morrison found that by introducing such transformations, the hundred million plus different string models operating in four, five, six, and ten space dimensions could all be united with perfect consistency into just one theory, the ten-dimensional one. To put it another way, theories formerly thought to be competing descriptions of reality—theories invoking "magnetic monopoles," "ordinary strings," "five-branes," "solitons," "type II strings," and "heterotic strings" (see box on page 27)—can all be integrated into a single, overarching theory.

Massless Black Holes?

As most students of science and viewers of *Star Trek* realize, a black hole has so much mass that its gravity pulls in anything—even light—that gets close enough to it. But for Strominger's black holes to fit neatly into string theory, black holes must become massless at critical moments. This necessity raises an obvious question: How can a black hole have zero mass without violating the definition of a black hole? Or more difficult yet, without violating the principles of gravity? Simply put, how can there be gravity without mass?

The answer was found in the spatial configuration of a black hole in extra dimensions. Strominger discovered that in six space dimensions, the mass of a particular black hole (an "extremal" black hole, one with a mass and charge so tiny as to be comparable to one of the fundamental particles) is proportional to its surface area. By making this area small enough, eventually the mass becomes zero. To answer the question another way, special relativity ($E = mc^2$) tells us mass and energy are interchangeable. General relativity extends this principle to space and time. When spatial lines are curled up tightly enough, mass and space become interchangeable. For the tiny black holes Strominger is describing, the space curvature is certainly tight enough to accomplish this interchangeability. As if this finding weren't exciting enough, Strominger also discovered that his extremal black holes become massless in precisely those circumstances—and only those circumstances—necessary to eliminate the remaining physical absurdities of string theory. Black holes, which never fit into string theory before, now do fit. And they fit in a way that actually solves string theory's most perplexing problems.

Experimental Evidences for Strings

Unquestionably, strings yield an amazingly elegant set of physical principles. They beautifully unite the physics of the very small with the physics of the very large. But do string theorists have any experimental or observational evidences to support their gorgeous equations? This claim that the universe began with ten dimensions (for a split second) and a unified set of physics forces is dramatic, but what verification, besides workable equations, can we see?

Evidences come from four areas of research. The first set comes from the particle accelerator experiments proving that two of the four forces of physics, the weak nuclear force and electromagnetism, are indeed unifiable. These kinds of experiments also give at least partial evidence that the strong nuclear force is unifiable with these other two. Though we do not yet have any experimental evidence to show that gravity is unifiable with the other three forces, a soon-to-be-operational gravity wave detector holds the potential to affirm this part of the theory.

While particle accelerators also provided proof for the existence of quarks and leptons, supersymmetry also predicts that for every fundamental particle of matter known as a *fermion*, a wavelike particle known as a *boson* must exist. These bosons mediate the fundamental forces of physics. While particle accelerator experiments have detected fermions and bosons in abundance, none has yet detected a matched fermion-boson pair, which supersymmetry calls for. But we know why such a detection has not been made: Experiments to date lack the power necessary to find a matched pair. The next generation of particle accelerators may have that power, perhaps as soon as the turn of the century.[43] (Such a detection would have been easy for the canceled superconducting supercollider.)

The third and arguably strongest category of evidence comes via experimental proofs for relativity theory. To be viable, string theory must yield the theories of both special and general relativity exactly as Einstein formulated them. If physicists had been able to discover string theory before they knew anything at all about relativity, both special and general relativity theory would have emerged easily and straightforwardly from the analysis of strings. Strings cannot move self-consistently throughout space and time unless relativity equations and principles are operating.

Thus, the experimental proofs that affirm special and general relativity simultaneously give evidence for the validity of string theory. Such proof has become more than adequate; it is staggering.

The work of Taylor's team affirmed general relativity to better than a trillionth of a percent precision, as you've already read. And even stronger evidence exists for special relativity; it has been affirmed to a precision of better than a ten millionth of a trillionth percent.[44] Because relativity is solidly established, so are the many components of string theory, including the ten space dimensions that link with relativity.

Additional strong confirmation comes from the unique role string theory plays in solving major mysteries of physics. All previous quantum field theories ruled out the possibility of gravity, and all gravitational theories were at a loss to explain the properties of quantum mechanics. In other words, if quantum mechanics were true, there should be no gravity. If gravity were true, there should be no quantum mechanics. And yet we possess overwhelming experimental evidence for the operation of both.

String theory is a quantum theory that demands the operation of gravity. It is the only theory that self-consistently explains all the known properties of the known fundamental particles (now numbering fifty-eight), all the properties and principles of quantum mechanics, all the properties and principles of both special and general relativity, the operation of all four forces of physics, and all the known details of the creation event.

To say that string theory represents a monumental development in physics, helping us to understand the natural realm and the awesome capacities of the God who created it, is to state the case mildly.

Dimensional Split

At the very heart of string theory is the proposal that the cosmos experienced a dimensional split at 10^{-43} seconds (a ten millionth of a trillionth of a trillionth of a trillionth of a second) after the creation event began. At that instant, the ten-dimensional expanding universe split into two: a six-dimensional piece that permanently ceased expanding and never produced matter, and a four-dimensional piece that became our dimensions of length, width, height, and time. That four-dimensional system continued to expand and eventually produced matter and stars (see figure 3.1).

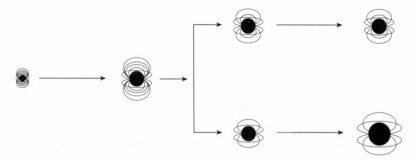

Figure 3.1: The Growth and Splitting of the Ten-Dimensional Universe
In the beginning (T = 0) the Creator brought into existence ten infinitely compressed dimensions. These ten dimensions uncurled, forming a larger and larger volume of 10-D space. At T = 10^{-43} seconds, the emerging universe splits into a 6-D piece and a 4-D piece. The six dimensions stop growing while the other four dimensions continue to expand, forming the universe in which we reside. (It is not possible to depict in this illustration that the six dimensions remain curled up around the other four.)

Another way of picturing this dimensional split is to see all the spatial dimensions of the universe originally curled up in a very tiny "superball." In the beginning, these spatial dimensions began to uncurl. At 10^{-43} seconds after the creation event, six of these dimensions stopped uncurling and the rest became our observable universe of gas, dust, galaxies, solar systems, etc. To this day, the six other dimensions remain curled up everywhere, at every location within our four dimensions of length, width, height, and time. An analogy for what happened would be to picture a sheet of paper so tightly curled up around one of its edges that it now appears to be a string or line. What was once a two-dimensional sheet of paper, a plane, would now look like a one-dimensional line since the second dimension is so tightly curled up around the first dimension as to disappear.

Extra Space Dimensions and God

The space-time theorem of general relativity establishes not only the Creator's extra time dimension(s) or their equivalent, but also His capacity to operate in all the space dimensions the universe has ever possessed (or their equivalent). What follows, then, from string theory and from all these recent findings in particle physics and astrophysics, is that God must be operating in a *minimum* of eleven dimensions of space and time (or their practical equivalent).

Why So Few Dimensions for Us?

We may be inclined to wonder why God limited our existence to just three space dimensions when we could have enjoyed some spectacular "advantages" by living in a few more. The Bible suggests that we will live in some of those dimensions some day, with Him (see chapter 17); but as it turns out, human life—our physical, carbon-based life—could not exist in a universe composed of any more (or fewer) than three expanding dimensions of space. The gravity that makes stable planetary systems possible, including the system that gives us the necessary temperature, atmosphere, day-night cycle, and other life-essential conditions, would render such systems impossible in a four- or more-dimensional system. (Gravity obeys an inverse square law in three space dimensions. Thus, the gravitational tug from a body drops to one quarter for every doubling of its distance. In four dimensions the force of gravity would drop to one eighth for every doubling of the body's distance. In five dimensions, it would drop to a sixteenth, and in six dimensions, to just a thirty-secondth.) Only if gravity obeys an inverse square law, as it does in three dimensions, are stable, approximately circular orbits possible.

Electromagnetism provides another reason for three space dimensions. In a system with anything other than three space dimensions, electrons would either spiral away from or spiral into the nuclei they orbit. In anything other than a large three-spatial-dimensional universe, neutral atoms (atoms with no charge) and molecules could never exist. Stable stars are possible because the electromagnetic forces in stars balance the gravitational forces, a condition met only in a large, three-dimensional system. Thus, atomic-based physical life—subject to gravity, thermodynamics, and electromagnetism—would be impossible in any universe but a three-space-dimensional one.

A home fit for our physical bodies can exist only in a space-time region composed of one large, uncurled dimension of time and three large, uncurled dimensions of space. The universe's dimensional makeup constitutes one of dozens of tangible evidences for purposeful cosmic design with life in mind (popularly known as the anthropic principle).[45] By definition alone, design demands a personal, intelligent, powerful Designer.

A Privileged Generation

Living on the brink of the twenty-first century may present us with some dreadful liabilities—social, political, and environmental crises, to mention a few. And yet, from a scientific and spiritual perspective, we can consider ourselves privileged.

We are the only people ever to see (or need) direct scientific proof not only for God's existence, but also for His transcendent capacity to create space and time dimensions, as well as to operate in dimensions independent from our own four. The remarkable advance of research reveals a God who lives and operates in the equivalent of at least eleven dimensions of space and time. Such extra-dimensional capacities are more than adequate to resolve the doctrinal conflicts and paradoxical issues that have divided the church and perplexed both believers and unbelievers for centuries.

To loosely paraphrase a verse of Scripture, "Where division, arrogance, and unbelief abound, humbling evidences do much more abound." That is God's grace.

CHAPTER FOUR

SCIENCE'S TETHERS

Breakthroughs pointing to a realm beyond the cosmos gave scientists an indescribable thrill. A few sailed past euphoria into a delusion of power and grandeur, with the hope of finding a "theory of everything," even "the mind of God."[1-3]

Such boasts arouse disdain and distrust among God-fearing people, and the temptation becomes strong to discount, if not utterly reject, these researchers' valuable achievements. Let us not make that mistake. While we can allow scientists some appropriate pride of accomplishment and heartily congratulate them, we can rest assured that their hope is futile—the Bible says so and so does science. Another set of discoveries—a less heralded set, to be sure— securely tethers our flights of fancy and our Babel-like inclinations.

While pushing past old boundaries, researchers have proven, ironically, that the theoretical limits on our ability to measure and understand are much more circumscribed than they had imagined. Rather than elevating human beings and demoting God, scientific discoveries do just the opposite. Reality allows less room than ever for glorifying humans and more than ever for glorifying God.

Unknowable Center

Through special relativity theory, scientists learned that no absolute reference system exists for measuring motions in space.[4] Through general relativity we learned one reason for that impossibility: the universe's matter and energy reside on the three-dimensional surface of a four-dimensional system.[5] These findings mean that we humans can never locate the center of the universe. We can only make measurements along its space-time surface.[6]

Figure 4.1: Two-Dimensional Creatures Residing on a Three-Dimensional Sphere
The three dimensions of the sphere are longitude, latitude, and radius. The creatures have no radius, only longitude and latitude. Living on the surface of the sphere, they can make measurements of longitude and latitude anywhere along the surface, but they can never detect or measure anything in the radius dimension. Though they could determine that their world has a center in a third dimension, they would never be able to locate that center.

Our situation is analogous to that of two-dimensional beings residing on the surface of a three-dimensional sphere (see figure 4.1). Their bodies extend over two dimensions only, length and width, or longitude and latitude. They have no thickness, no radius dimension. They can make length and width measurements only. Even though they may be able, through careful study, to determine that their physical environment is a three-dimensional globe, they will never be able to determine where they are relative to the center of the globe. Likewise, we cannot determine where we are relative to the center of the universe. The only advantage we have over the 2-D creatures on a 3-D globe is that our 4-D surface is growing, and we 3-D creatures can measure that growth. Thus, we can determine more easily that our system has some kind of center. But the actual location remains hidden from us. Only a four- (or more-) dimensional being can see it.

Uncertainty Principle

Researchers have always acknowledged that the certainty of their measurements is limited by the precision (or imprecision) of their measuring tools. In 1925 Werner Heisenberg discovered that even with perfect instruments, a fundamental limitation remains. According to Heisenberg's uncertainty principle, we cannot accurately measure both a particle's position and momentum (mass times velocity).[7-8] The more accurately we choose to measure the position of an electron, for example, the less accurately we will be able to measure the electron's momentum, and vice versa. If we were to measure the position of an electron to within a millionth of an inch, we could determine that electron's position one second later to an accuracy no more precise than 1,500 miles!

Since the 1920s, the measuring limits implied by Heisenberg's uncertainty principle have been confirmed by countless experiments.[9] A certain amount of ignorance for the human observer is fundamentally built into the sub-microscopic world of quantum mechanics (the realm in which energy is not infinitely divisible). Though God can describe all the properties of quantum particles and quantum events, humans cannot.

Thermodynamic Limitations

One corollary of the big bang model and of general relativity says that the universe is "thermodynamically closed." No energy or matter from any other thermodynamic system can flow into ours, nor can energy or matter from ours flow into it, at least not during the universe's knowable history. All the universe's matter and energy remain confined to the universe's space-time dimensions. Thus we humans are confined in our measuring and detecting abilities to our universe's space-time "envelope." If any other universe exists, we cannot make contact with it or detect its existence. Its space-time envelope cannot overlap ours.

Built into the inflationary hot big bang model[10] is yet another knowledge boundary. If the universe did indeed undergo a brief period of hyper-expansion roughly 10^{-35} (0.00000000000000000000 00000000000001) seconds after the initial creation event, this hyper-rapid expansion effectively washed out much, if not all, information about what was happening in the universe before that moment.

A practical limitation on our ability to probe the early cosmos also exists. As the universe expands, it cools. The closer we get to the creation event, the higher the universe's temperature. The only way to directly test early conditions is to recreate extremely high temperatures with the help of particle accelerators.[11-12] But to duplicate the conditions present at 10^{-35} seconds would require a particle accelerator more than forty trillion miles long. Since our resources for building instruments will always be limited, there will always be at least a tiny time period about which we must remain ignorant. Again, God knows, but we cannot.

Incompleteness Theorem

In 1931 Austrian mathematician Kurt Gödel established that mathematical "truths" exist for which we can develop no absolutely rigorous proofs. No set of axioms can be proven totally consistent. No set of axioms, then, is provably complete.

Gödel's discovery became known as the incompleteness theorem, for it meant that mathematicians must accept a minimum level of incompleteness in their "facts." The ramifications of Gödel's theorem reach beyond mathematics. The theorem also imposes a minimum incompleteness on our theories of physics and our knowledge of the universe.

This principle of incompleteness will be reflected in whatever model of origins proves most accurate in describing our universe's origin and characteristics. We humans can never discover and state all the truths about the universe or demonstrate the totality of its consistency. Perfect insight into the physics of the cosmos will always remain beyond our capability. However much we come to know about the universe, we will not be able to discover a "theory of everything," for no rational models of the universe can be proven totally consistent and complete. As God chooses what to reveal to us through the Bible, so also He chooses what to reveal to us through His creation, the "words" He declares through the heavens and the earth.[13] In the words of Moses, "The secret things belong to the LORD our God, but the things revealed belong to us and to our children forever."[14]

Plenty of "Things Revealed"

The "things revealed" deserve our attention, our probing to the maximum extent of human capability. What thrills and challenges researchers in virtually every discipline is that every discovery opens yet another door for exploration. What we learn shows us how much more there is to learn.

The limits on our abilities to know truth and visualize truth merely remind us that we are the creatures, not the Creator. But the limits do not stop us from seeking to gain a clearer picture of who He is through studying both His inspired Word and His creative work. Each will reveal His glory in its own way. Even if the windows through which we gaze on His realm have a few ripples and dark spots in them, we will be awed at the majestic beauty we see. He has left the curtains open. He invites us to look in.

CHAPTER FIVE

EXTRA DIMENSIONS IN THE BIBLE

A few thousand years before physicists conceived of general relativity, the space-time theorem, quarks, supersymmetry, unified field theories, and vibrating strings, a written document described extra-dimensional reality. That document is the Bible. While the marshaling of the scientific and philosophical wherewithal to discover the existence of dimensions beyond length, width, height, and time must rank as one of the greatest human achievements of the twentieth century, far more amazing is the Bible writers' depiction of phenomena in dimensions beyond the length, width, height, and time humans can experience or mentally picture. Mere imagination would be incapable of such a feat; and indeed, no other book previous to the modern era describes phenomena in dimensions independent of our four.

Beginning of Time

The first scholars to speak about the beginning of time were not Stephen Hawking and Roger Penrose, but rather Moses, the apostle Paul, and whoever wrote Hebrews. Genesis 1:1 boldly declares, "In the beginning God created the heavens and the earth." The phrase, "heavens and the earth," is translated from a combination of Hebrew nouns, which together refer to the entire physical universe.[1-2] The verb for "created" suggests the origin of something totally new, something that did not previously exist or that was previously undetectable.[3] The book of Hebrews provides this clarification: "By faith we understand that the universe was formed at

God's command, so that what is seen was not made out of what was visible."[4] To paraphrase, the cosmos we *can* detect came from that which lies *beyond* our ability to detect. These biblical statements declare that a transcendent Being created the cosmos, One who operates in a reality beyond our matter, energy, space, and time.

Specific mention of God's transcendent time dimension appears in the New Testament epistles:

> This grace was given us in Christ Jesus before the beginning of time.[5] . . . God, who does not lie, promised [the hope of eternal life] before the beginning of time.[6]

Paul states here that our time dimension had a beginning and implies that God created our time dimension. These verses tell us that God engaged in cause and effect behavior before our time dimension existed. Thus, there must be at least the equivalent of a second dimension of time for God.

Other biblical passages refer to God's activities before He created the universe, often translated "the world":

> The LORD brought me [Wisdom] forth as the first of his works, before his deeds of old; I was appointed from eternity, from the beginning, before the world began.[7]

> "And now, Father, glorify me in your presence with the glory I had with you before the world began. . . . You loved me before the creation of the world."[8]

> He chose us . . . before the creation of the world.[9]

> He was chosen before the creation of the world.[10]

Most Bible scholars agree that "world" in these contexts refers to the totality of God's physical creation.[11-12] Again the Bible claims that God caused certain effects—He appointed, glorified, and made choices—before bringing the universe, including our time dimension, into existence.

The beginning of matter, energy, and even non-physical entities, is declared in these two passages:

> Through him all things were made; without him nothing
> was made that has been made.[13]

> For by him all things were created: things in heaven and on
> earth, visible and invisible, whether thrones or powers or
> rulers or authorities; all things were created by him and for
> him. He is before all things, and in him all things hold
> together.[14]

More than seventy-five Scripture verses affirm that the universe
had a beginning and that God created it.[15]

Contrasting Time Frames

According to the Bible, God can operate both apart from our time
frame and within it. But God's time realm gives Him a different perspective on time and a different experience of it:

> For a thousand years in your sight are like a day that has
> just gone by.[16]

In past centuries some scholars interpreted this verse concretely,
concluding that God's clock runs precisely 365,242 times slower
than ours.[17] In fact, whole theological systems have been built on
this interpretation. One group insists that God created the heavens
and the earth in six consecutive thousand-year "days" and that the
return of Jesus Christ must occur exactly 6,000 years after the creation of Adam.

However, the metaphoric intent of this verse (Psalm 90:4) seems
obvious from the context. The verse also compares a thousand years
to a "watch in the night," which means four hours in Old Testament
times and three in New Testament times. In other words, what
seems a long time to us can be a short time to God.

Peter suggests an even broader interpretation of this verse when
he writes, "With the Lord a day is like a thousand years, and a thou-

sand years are like a day."[18] Peter means here that God can experience the passing of time more quickly or more slowly than we humans do. He has the capacity to experience time at any rate He chooses.

This biblical claim makes sense if God operates along one or more time dimensions independent of ours (see figure 5.1).

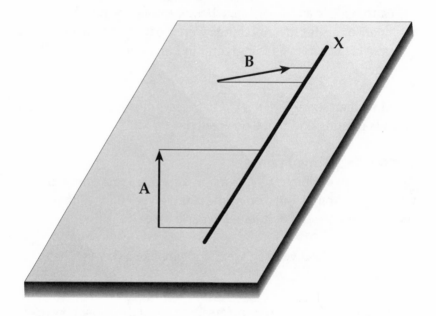

Figure 5.1: God's Time Versus Our Time
In two or more time dimensions, God could choose to operate along a variety of time lines, such as **A** and **B**. Though **A** and **B** have equal length, if we superimpose them on our time line (**X**), we would experience **A** as much longer than **B**.

Extra Space Dimensionality

In many biblical passages God manifests Himself in our dimensions in ways that seem strange to human observers. He speaks to Moses from a burning bush that does not burn up. The Israelites see Him in a pillar of cloud by day and of fire by night. His voice hits their ears like thunderclaps. God's "finger" inscribes the Ten Commandments in stone.

As astonishing as these encounters must have been, imagine

the disciples' amazement when Jesus came to them bodily, after His crucifixion, without opening the locked doors or windows of their hideout. Both Luke and John record the event:

> On the evening of that first day of the week, when the disciples were together, with the doors locked for fear of the Jews, Jesus came and stood among them. . . . They were startled and frightened, thinking they saw a ghost. He said to them, "Why are you troubled, and why do doubts rise in your minds? Look at my hands and my feet. It is I myself! Touch me and see; a ghost does not have flesh and bones, as you see I have."
>
> When he had said this, he showed them his hands and feet. And while they still did not believe it because of joy and amazement, he asked them, "Do you have anything here to eat?" They gave him a piece of broiled fish, and he took it and ate it in their presence.[19]

The disciples' shock arises not only from their inability to comprehend how Jesus could be alive and present but also from their knowledge that physical objects cannot pass through physical barriers without damage to either the object or the barrier. No wonder they concluded that Jesus must be a ghost! What they saw made no sense to them.

Jesus responded to their perplexity by demonstrating His physicality. He invited their touch, confirming that He had the solidity of flesh and bones.[20] He ate food from their table, further affirming His physical reality.[21]

The disciples could not know at that moment they had seen an example of what is possible for someone who has access to extra space dimensions. They had not seen a film depicting how a ball can turn inside out without breaking its surface, given four space dimensions. They could not understand that when an object can rotate into extra space dimensions, what are barriers to us can prove to be no problem to the object. That is because each rotation can reduce, by one, the number of dimensions that present themselves to the object as a barrier.

Figure 5.2 demonstrates this principle of dimensionality reduction. A two-dimensional rectangle can be rotated from its position in the dimensions of length and width into a third dimension of depth. A three-dimensional observer facing the axis of rotation from far away in the depth dimension would see the rectangle shrink in its length dimension until it becomes a line. If a fourth dimension of space existed, the rectangle could be rotated about another axis from its position in the width and depth dimensions into a new position located in the depth dimension plus a fourth dimension. The same observer would see the "line" transform into a "point." From his or her perspective, the rectangle has lost both its length and width dimensions.

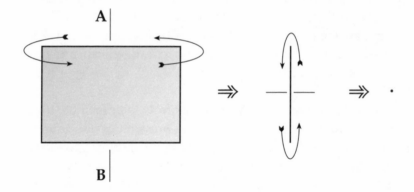

Figure 5.2: Transforming a Rectangle into a Point
The two-dimensional rectangle on the left rotates about an axis (**AB**) into a third dimension of depth. It now appears to us three-dimensional observers as a line only. If the rectangle were to rotate again into a fourth space dimension, that line would appear to us as a point only.

Jesus would have no problem passing through the walls of that locked room with His physical body if He were simply to rotate His body into extra dimensions of space. For example, He could have rotated the first dimension of His physical body from spatial dimension one into spatial dimension four. He could have rotated the second dimension of His physical body from spatial dimension two into spatial dimension five. And He could have rotated the third dimension of His physical body from spatial dimension three into spatial dimension six. His physical body would then have been present in dimensions four, five, and six and absent from the disciples' dimensions one, two, and three. Since the walls of the upper room are in dimensions one, two, and three, they would no longer pose a barrier to Jesus' physical body. He would have no trouble moving into the upper room without disturbing the walls or doors. Once inside the upper room, He could have rotated His physical body from spatial dimensions four, five, and six back into dimensions one, two, and three, where the disciples could see, hear, and touch Him.

This six-dimension rotation scenario may explain how Jesus entered the upper room to meet with His disciples after rising from the dead, or He may have chosen a different approach entirely. The point is not to assert one explanation above others but rather to suggest that His multidimensional capabilities offer Him countless ways to accomplish the feat—and the feat itself more than hints at His extra-dimensionality.

Other Extra-Dimensional Miracles

Miracles described in the Bible seem to fit into one of two categories. The first category includes natural events occurring with supernatural timing or supernatural placement or both. The event itself is not unnatural, but when and where it occurs is. The second encompasses supernatural events, phenomena that defy the physical laws of the universe.

As an example of the first type of miracle, God fulfilled His promise to deliver Jerusalem from Assyria's siege when thousands of King Sennacherib's soldiers fell ill and died in one night.[22] We are familiar with people dying of an ailment; but when several thousand previously healthy soldiers die overnight from an illness at a critical moment in the siege, we are astonished.

The second type of miracle represents the biblical revelation of a transcendent, extra-dimensional God, and Scripture offers many examples of such miracles, "transportation" phenomena among them:

+ Elijah's ministry ends with a death-defying ride to heaven in what appears to Elisha as a chariot of fire.[23]

+ Philip is sent by an angel to explain the gospel to an
  Ethiopian eunuch in Gaza and immediately afterward
  arrives in Azotus.[24]
+ Jesus glows with blinding light as He converses on a
  mountaintop with Moses and Elijah, who had left this
  earth many centuries earlier.[25]

Miracles such as the backward movement of the shadow on
Hezekiah's sundial also describe extra-dimensional phenomena.
Since the miracle was witnessed in Jerusalem and acknowledged
in far-flung regions,[26] neither local atmospheric conditions nor misreading nor malfunctions of sundials offer reasonable explanations.
Nor does reversal of the earth's rotation or the sun's sudden leap
from its position, for both events would be sufficiently wrenching
to destroy all life on Earth. The more reasonable conclusion is that
God intervened from beyond our space-time dimensions.

In the account of Jesus and Peter walking on water, we see a
violation of gravity, among other physical laws. Some force from
beyond matter, energy, and our space-time dimensions held the two
men above the waves.

Though self-declared seers always have been around, seeking
to make a name and a fortune by their supposed powers of prog-
nostication, none has proved reliable even to 50 percent accuracy.
Even that percentage is bumped up by the tendency toward ambi-
guity and short-range prediction. But what more can be expected of
humans restricted to a single time line where time proceeds forward
only? That God's spokesmen can precisely describe all manner of
future events[27] proves His time capabilities go beyond the linear.

The book of Revelation goes so far as to predict the eventual
replacement of the entire universe and all its physical laws and
space-time structures. The apostle John's description of the new
heavens and earth requires the operation of new physical laws—
distinct from gravity, thermodynamics, and electromagnetism—
and a different dimensional matrix (see chapter 17). And, since all
spirit beings survive the elimination and replacement of the familiar dimensional domain, these beings must reside—at that
moment—in an extra-dimensional realm.

Christ's Dimensional Sacrifice

Jesus Christ's incarnation and resurrection represent the most dramatic and significant expressions of God's extra-dimensional capacities. A succinct description appears in the book of Philippians.[28]

In coming to Earth as an embryo in the virgin's womb, Christ "emptied" Himself, leaving behind the extra-dimensional realm and capacities He shared with God the Father and God the Holy Spirit. When He had completed the work He set out to do, the work of redemption, He returned to the place and the powers He had left behind. The magnitude of this dimensional (or equivalent) sacrifice staggers human imagination (see chapters 9 and 10).

Though the illustration pales by comparison, consider what it would be like for us to lose just one dimension, to enter a two-dimensional realm, even for an hour, inviting two-dimensional "beings" to come with us to our three-dimensional realm of shapes, colors, sounds, tastes, and countless experiences—and *truths*—unimaginable to them. If we cared for them as God cares for us, we would gently and often remind them that help is on the way. A special tutor—the Holy Spirit—is available at every moment to guide them in understanding, trusting, and applying these promises and truths.

CHAPTER SIX

EXTRA-DIMENSIONAL DOCTRINES

In addition to the direct biblical evidences of God's extra-dimensional intervention in our four-dimensional realm, the Bible presents doctrines that can make sense only if extra dimensions, or their equivalent, exist. Such doctrines represent one of the Bible's great distinctives. They provide evidence of divine inspiration, for they defy human imagination and visualization. Other holy books include contradictions that cannot be resolved in extra dimensions, and many religious cults attempt to explain all biblical doctrines in a four-dimensional context. These reflect human thinking, which both the Bible and science say will always fall short of God's.

The Rut of the Familiar

Extra-dimensional thinking is difficult for most people, especially for adults. Age seems to lock our minds in a four-dimensional rut. One reason may be that the older we become, the farther removed we are from the transition we made in infancy from two-dimensional perception to three-dimensional. Until we are at least a few months old, we have difficulty distinguishing between life-sized photographs and real people or objects. Our brains need some practice at transforming two-dimensional images into three-dimensional forms and distinguishing which is which. The longer ago we made this transition from 2-D to 3-D spatial thinking, the more difficult we may find the transition to the further steps of 4-D, 5-D, and more-D thinking.

Contradictions, Antinomies, and Paradoxes

Because physicists work with paradoxes and dimensionality all the time, they have ready access to terms and concepts that are needed in applying the new cosmological findings to issues beyond science. Unfortunately, these terms and concepts are rarely, if ever, taught in seminaries, where theologians, pastors, and other Christian leaders receive professional training.

Here is a brief overview of some key terms and their definitions (see box on page 53 for more complete definitions):

Contradiction: a direct and unresolvable opposition between two statements, laws, or principles.

Paradox: a direct but resolvable opposition between two true statements, laws, or principles.

Antinomy: a direct contradiction between two statements, laws, or principles that seem equally true and necessary.

Recognizing the apparent contradictory nature of certain biblical doctrines, Bible students often struggle to find some way to adjust the texts, the terms, or the concepts, and end up with the discomfort of accepting what does not make sense. Some give up their trust in the accuracy and authority of God's Word, choosing which parts to accept and which to reject, while others simply redefine "inspiration."

Those who hold fast to their view of Scripture as the true and trustworthy Word of God often resort to treating these problematic doctrines as "antinomies," and the results are painful. Christians' approach to the doctrine of humanity's free will versus God's sovereignty provides an example. The Bible teaches God has total control over everything, including all our decisions and actions. It also teaches we have moment-by-moment freedom—and responsibility—in making decisions and taking action. As J. I. Packer points out, the Puritan tradition acknowledges both statements as undeniably true and yet undeniably contradictory.[1] Since a hallmark of the Christian faith is its freedom from contradiction,[2-3] Puritans and others inevitably chose sides, some upholding predestination and denying free will, others upholding free will and denying predestination. The church splintered over the issue. Tragically, people even killed others over it.

WHAT'S THE DIFFERENCE?

Many people confuse or equate paradoxes with contradictions or antinomies. Yet important distinctions exist among the three terms.

Contradiction: direct opposition between statements, conclusions, laws, or principles so that it remains impossible for the statements, conclusions, laws, or principles being compared to both be true at the same time, in the same location, and in the same context. An example would be the people of Jerusalem at one instant concluding that Jesus was not the Messiah because they knew where He came from and at another instant concluding He was not the Messiah because they did not know where He came from.[4]

Antinomy: opposition or a contradiction between statements, conclusions, laws, or principles that seem equally logical, reasonable, or necessary. An example would be the Puritan conclusion that both human free will and divine predestination are undeniably true and yet undeniably contradictory.[5]

Paradox: an apparent contradiction; something that seems like a contradiction but has at least the possibility of resolution when examined in all possibly existing time, space, and contextual frames of reference. An example would be a man aging only thirty years as he makes a round trip at relativistic velocity to the Andromeda Galaxy while back home the earth would experience the passing of four million years.[6]

If only Christian leaders had recognized the "contradiction" for what it is, a paradox, the church could have avoided untold damage and heartache. If only they had trusted God's "higher ways" and "higher thoughts" while awaiting further research and insight, wasted energies and lives could have been profitably invested in the advance of the gospel.

Tools for Resolving Paradoxes
One wonderful advantage of being alive today is that astronomers and physicists have given us both the faith-supporting verification

of God's supernatural capacities and the methods for using this new information to resolve faith-shattering conflicts. Their investigation of the physical realm has enabled them to distinguish paradoxes from contradictions and to discover what works and what does not work in unraveling paradoxes. The eight basic tools they have developed work as well on biblical and philosophical problems as they do on physical ones. Applied either singly or in combination, these tools always succeed:

1. Establish the correct frame(s) of reference or point(s) of view for measuring or observing the phenomena in question.
2. Establish the correct definition(s) and context(s) of the system(s) under investigation.
3. Identify correctly and completely the initial and final conditions of the phenomena in question.
4. Gather more information about the circumstances in which the phenomena occur.
5. Make more precise measurements.
6. Make measurements over a larger or smaller range of magnitude (e.g., over a longer or shorter time span or distance).
7. Make measurements over different dimensions.
8. Calculate or discern the effects of dimensions or realms in which human measurements cannot (yet) be made.

Though these precepts sound more scientific and mathematical than theological, they are equally effective when applied to biblical paradoxes; it just takes some practice. Before we begin making these applications, though, I must add one more tool to the list.

God's capacities may supersede cause and effect endeavors along dimensional lines, even along an infinite number of dimensional lines. Since God has demonstrated the capacity to create space-time dimensions, He may have at His disposal super dimensions that encompass space-time capacities and much more, or He may possess transdimensional attributes that somehow permit cause and effect endeavors independent of space-time dimensions.

Such speculations as yet lie beyond human discovery. So, we will continue to explore what has been discovered and what such discoveries can do to strengthen the faith and enhance the oneness of Christians around the world.

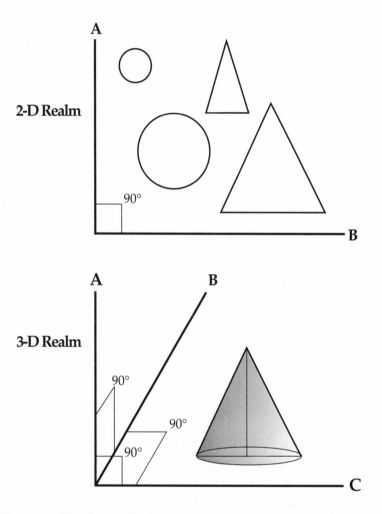

Figure 6.1: Triangles and Circles in Two and Three Dimensions of Space
In a two-dimensional realm, triangles cannot be equivalent to circles in any context. But in a three-dimensional realm, an isosceles triangle (for example) could be rotated about its axis to form a cone. This triangle could be described as a series of concentric circles with progressively smaller diameters rising from the base of the triangle to its vertex.

Triangles and Circles

Resolution of most biblical paradoxes requires application of more than one of the eight tools listed above. To prepare for tackling such complex cases, we can practice on some simple, physical paradoxes, ones that a single tool can fix.

For example, we can resolve this seemingly contradictory set of statements: Triangles cannot be circles, and triangles can be circles. Given two dimensions of space, we take it as an obvious fact that triangles are never circles, and circles are never triangles. After all, triangles always have corners and circles never do. From this perspective, the second of the two statements seems blatantly incorrect, if not crazy. But in reality—three-dimensional reality—the second statement is as correct and rational as the first. In three space dimensions we can stand the triangle up on its base, bringing its length into the height dimension, spin the triangle around on its height axis, and thereby transcribe a cone (see figure 6.1). Since a cone is a series of concentric circles with progressively smaller diameters rising from the base to the vertex, a triangle can be equal to a circle in a three-dimensional context. There, the truth of both statements about triangles and circles can be recognized.

From a two-dimensional perspective, all we can perceive is one side of the paradox, namely that triangles are not circles. Whereas from our three-spatial-dimensional perspective we can visualize the contexts of both sides of the paradox. Plane dwellers, or flat-landers, could use higher dimensional mathematics to demonstrate that the paradox is resolvable in three spatial dimensions, but without some evidence for the existence of the extra dimension, they would probably not think of that approach right away, nor could they gain a visual grasp of the different contexts that make the paradox resolvable.

Do Logic Rules Change in Extra Dimensions?

The rules of logic do not change as one travels from one specific dimensional system to another. They do, however, become more difficult or complicated to apply and test.

The law of causality can be used as an illustration. This law says that every effect must have a cause, and that effects emanate from their causes. For beings experiencing one time dimension only, cause and effect phenomena always will proceed along that single time line. If time cannot stop or reverse, causes must always precede their effects. If the arrow of time could be reversed, however, causes could precede or follow their effects.

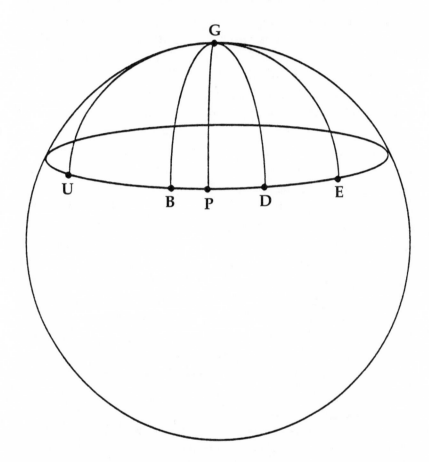

Figure 6.2: God's Operations in a Sphere of Time
In three dimensions of time, or the equivalent, God could generate causes anywhere within, on, or outside of the sphere. The line segment **UE** represents the time dimension for the universe. At point **U** the universe comes into existence. At point **E** its existence ends. **B** is the birth date for an individual human. **D** is his or her time of death, and **P** the present moment. God, from a single point or instant of time, say **G**, could simultaneously generate causes at points **U, B, P, D,** and **E** along our time line.

In two dimensions of time, a particular cause and effect process that would take a fixed period to transpire in one time dimension could occur over an arbitrarily long or brief period (including infinitely long and infinitely brief) along other time lines in the time plane (see figure 5.1, page 44).

In three time dimensions, a being could simultaneously generate effects in the past, the present, and the future of a one-time-dimensional being (see figure 6.2). Though the law of causality remains the same in all four of these dimensional situations, its application can produce radically different results.

Basic arithmetic provides another illustration. Switching geometric systems may seem to change the rules, but it does not. In Euclidean (plane) geometry, the shortest distance between two points is a straight line. In non-Euclidean (curved) geometry, the shortest distance may be an arc. San Francisco and Tokyo, for example, are measured to be about 5,225 miles in non-Euclidean geometry (measured along the earth's surface) but only 4,853 miles apart in Euclidean geometry (cutting a straight line through the interior of the earth). When we present the two statements side by side, San Francisco and Tokyo are 5,225 miles apart and 4,853 miles apart, the arithmetic value of the mile appears to have changed, but it has not. Only our geometric perspective has changed.

In extra dimensions of time and space, rules of logic—including rules of morality—remain consistent. They do not change or bend or twist. Yet the geometric axioms we use and the capacities available to accomplish certain tasks surely do.

Paradox Avoidance and Heresy

Some Bible scholars express concern that approaching biblical difficulties as paradoxes opens a door to heresy. It can lead to error if we mistake a non-paradoxical problem for a paradoxical one or if we misapply the tools for paradox resolution. In either case, careful scholarship, meticulously reviewed, offers a vital safeguard. So does training and practice in identifying and resolving paradoxes. The more experience we gain in working with paradoxes, the more easily and accurately we will be able to identify them and the more adept we will become at resolving them.

Must We Think So Hard?

For many of us, perhaps the greatest resistance to exploring extra-dimensional doctrines and employing the tools of paradox resolution comes from our hesitancy to exercise our brains. Though none of the thinking processes required for extra-dimensional forays requires a high IQ, their complexity and our inability to make concrete mental pictures demands greater mental focus and mental discipline than we may typically practice. But the rewards are also greater.

Worshiping the Lord with more of our mind can only enhance our capacity to worship Him with our heart, soul, and strength (Deuteronomy 6:5 and Matthew 22:37). In that spirit, let's now take a look at some of the paradoxical biblical doctrines that have mystified Christians and nonChristians for centuries.

CHAPTER SEVEN

GOD AND EXTRA TIME DIMENSIONS

If God does operate in at least one extra dimension of time, what does this tell us about God's capabilities beyond creating the universe and us? What we have seen so far has laid a foundation to answer some mystifying questions about God raised by children and scholars alike.

Whatever campus I visit, from grade school to graduate school, two questions come up more frequently than any others. The first is: If God created us, who created God? Children ask this question with obvious sincerity as they seek to affirm their emerging comprehension of time and cause and effect. Skeptical scholars sometimes ask without listening for an answer. They raise the question as an impossible stumper, as justification for their agnostic stance.

For anyone willing to stretch his or her mind a little, an answer is available, one that represents both the truth of Scripture and the facts of nature. Both sources affirm that the universe, with everything it contains, is confined to a single time line (or dimension) and is further confined to moving in one direction along that line. Even if we were to experience the stretching, or dilation, of time by moving at velocities approaching the speed of light, we could neither stop nor reverse time's arrow. The question of God's beginning reflects our understanding of these principles: Whatever exists has a starting point along the line of time and was caused by something or someone with an earlier starting point. In other words, any entity confined to a single line of time, in which time cannot be stopped or reversed, must have a moment of beginning or creation.

An uncaused effect, a beginningless anything or anyone, contradicts our experiential knowledge of reality—but not reality itself. For both the Bible and scientific investigation present us with the reality of a Being who has the capacity to create our time dimension and fix its direction, a Being who possesses apparently unlimited time capacities.

For our limited imagination's sake, however, we can consider what is possible for Him in a two-dimensional time frame, which would constitute a time plane. Just how many time dimensions, or their equivalent, God accesses we do not know, but we do have theoretical, observational, and theological proofs for these two dimensions.

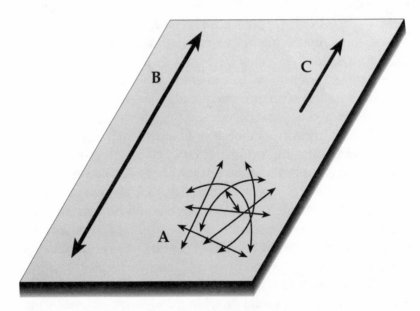

Figure 7.1: An Uncreated God in Two Time Dimensions
If time were two-dimensional rather than one-dimensional, it would be some kind of plane rather than a line. If this were the case, one could have an infinite number of time lines (**A**) running in an infinite number of directions. This, according to general relativity and the Bible, is the situation with the Creator. If the Creator were to so choose, He could move and operate for infinite time, forwards and backwards, on a time line (**B**) that never intersects or touches the time line of our universe (**C**). As such, He would have no beginning and no end. He would not be created.

As figure 7.1 (page 62) shows, a plane of time offers the possibility of an infinite number of time lines running in an infinite number of directions. God has the capacity, thus, to move and operate backwards and forwards along an infinitely long time line, or along as many time lines, infinite or otherwise, as He chooses. He can operate, if He desires, on a time line parallel to our time line or on one intersecting our time line, but He is not compelled to do either. Thus, God has the capacity to cause effects for infinite time on innumerable time lines that never intersect or touch our time line. As such, we could point to no beginning and no end for Him. Since beginnings only make sense where time in some way is linear, God must be a beginningless Being. He has always existed and will always remain. He never had a creation event.

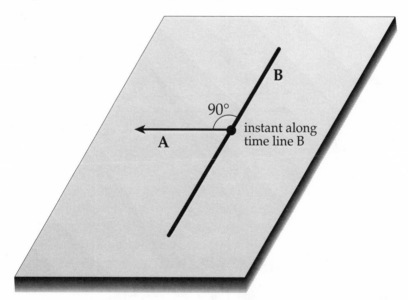

Figure 7.2: Infinite Time at an Instant of Time
In a plane of time, time line **A** can proceed for as long as one desires while in an independent dimension or line of time, **B**, time is not progressing at all. The first time line, **A**, simply needs to be perpendicular, or at a right angle (in Euclidean geometries), to the second line, **B**.

This illustration helps us to picture more clearly how the words of John 1:3 and Colossians 1:16-17 can be true. Just this one extra time dimension releases Him from the necessity of a beginning—

and an ending, for that matter. As these verses declare, He and He alone was not created.

Tuning in to Simultaneous Prayers

Anyone who has tried to listen to two or three conversations at once will guess what the second question is: How can God hear and respond to my prayers while millions or even billions of other people are praying at the same moment around the world? Again, our experience with time and attention tells us that no one can tune in to billions of voices at the same moment, much less respond to them all. As one third-grader stated the situation, a billion simultaneous calls would jam up God's phone line.

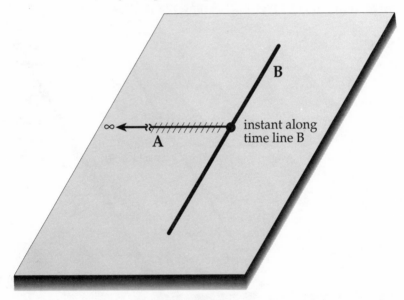

Figure 7.3: Listening to Six Billion Simultaneous Prayers
In a time line perpendicular to ours, God, for example, could divide up two billion hours into six billion twenty-minute segments. What is a mere instant for us could be two billion hours, or even an infinite amount of time for Him. Thus, God can easily pay attention and respond to the entire human race praying to Him at the same time.

Because of our confinement to a single, unidirectional, unstoppable time line, we humans are forced to communicate with other individuals (or groups) sequentially. But God does not live with such confinement. In a two-dimensional time plane such as the one described above, His capacity to communicate with any number of individuals simultaneously can be demonstrated. In this plane, God can extend a time line perpendicularly, or at a right angle, to our time line at any given moment along our time line (see figure 7.2, page 63). On this perpendicular line, God can give individual, undivided attention to any number of prayers simultaneously. None of us have any need to worry that our communication with Him will be drowned out by the communication of others (see figure 7.3, page 64).

Operating in a time plane is one provable way God could give individual attention to six billion simultaneous prayers. But, as the Master and Creator of at least ten space-time dimensions, He obviously would have many more options.

This simple illustration goes far in reassuring us that God really is attentive to us at every moment, in every situation. It gives new meaning to King David's expression of joy and wonder:

How precious to me are your thoughts, O God!
How vast is the sum of them!
Were I to count them, they would outnumber
     the grains of sand.[1]

Timefulness Versus Timelessness

My choice of the word *timeful* to describe God's time-related capacities deliberately contradicts a notion that much of the church has held and taught for many centuries, the notion of a "timeless" eternity as the realm where God lives and where we will live someday also. Timelessness seems to contradict both biblical and scientific evidences for the reality beyond our universe.

Plato first introduced the concept.[2] He reasoned that since all time-dependent phenomena are temporal, then to some degree they must be illusory and valueless, for only what is timeless, unchanging, and eternal retains ultimate reality and value.

Eight hundred years later, Saint Augustine incorporated Plato's concept into his interpretation of Christian doctrine.[3] Augustine noted that the Bible teaches God's independent, transcendent existence; that is, God lives apart from and beyond the limits of His creation. Since time is a component of the physical universe (the creation), Augustine correctly positioned the Creator outside the universe's time frame. To Augustine, this positioning meant God lives outside of time altogether, that is, in timelessness.

Eight centuries later, Saint Thomas Aquinas expanded on Augustine's interpretation of God's transcendence.[4] God's transcendence, he claimed, demanded the attributes of perfection, omnipotence, omniscience, omnipresence, spacelessness, and timelessness.

In the centuries since, Augustine and Aquinas's teachings have so dominated centers of theological scholarship that rare indeed is the student or professor who dares to challenge the doctrine of God's dwelling in a timeless eternity. Ironically, the notion of spacelessness is rarely, if ever, mentioned. Some scholars see this doctrine of God's timelessness as an essential element of orthodoxy. What Augustine, Aquinas, and other theologians have failed to grasp is that time, or its equivalent, could exist in something other than the time dimension of the cosmos.

The difficulty arose, and still arises, from a limited perspective on what "time" means. Time and causality are inextricably intertwined. Time is defined by the operation of cause-and-effect phenomena. It does not necessarily follow, however, that all causation occurs within the arena of a time coordinate as we humans experience it. Again, God may possess super-dimensions, capacities, or attributes that permit causation just as a time coordinate does. Attributing complete timelessness to God, though, means He exists where causes and effects do not happen, and this idea contradicts biblical teachings. To be fair, Augustine and Aquinas probably did not see the connection between time and cause and effect to the degree that people in contemporary society do. These philosophers probably would be shocked to discover that for many today timelessness connotes perfect inactivity and infinite boredom. Perhaps we can see from this connotation why so many people, both children and adults, have difficulty not only picturing but also anticipating heaven. That God is there and that we will dwell with Him in person helps stir our desire to be there, but beyond that, timelessness suggests a kind of motionlessness that strikes us as less than compelling or inviting.

We all like to be in neutral once in a while, but only to refuel our engines for jumping back into action. Personally, I can hardly wait to discover what type of multiple-time-dimensioned action God has in store for our unendingly timeful life with Him.

CHAPTER EIGHT

EXTRA-DIMENSIONALITY
AND GOD'S PROXIMITY

G od's nearness to us, His constant awareness of everything about us, is woven like a thread throughout the Bible. The reminders are pervasive, from Genesis to Revelation, as the following abbreviated list of references shows:

You are the God who sees me.[1]

Surely the LORD is in this place.[2]

The LORD searches every heart and understands every motive behind the thoughts.[3]

You [Lord] alone know the hearts of men.[4]

He [God] knows the way that I take.[5]

His [God's] eyes are on their ways.[6]

Does he [God] not see my ways and count my every step?[7]

His eyes are on the ways of men; he sees their every step. There is no dark place, no deep shadow, where evildoers can hide. God has no need to examine men further, that they should come before him for judgment. . . . He takes note of their deeds.[8]

The LORD looks down and sees all mankind; from his dwelling place he watches all who live on earth—he who forms the hearts of all, who considers everything they do.[9]

The LORD is close.[10]

He [God] knows the secrets of the heart.[11]

The LORD knows the thoughts of man.[12]

Yet you are near, O LORD. . . . All my ways are known to you.[13]

O LORD, you have searched me and you know me. You know when I sit and when I rise; you perceive my thoughts from afar. You discern my going out and my lying down; you are familiar with all my ways. Before a word is on my tongue you know it completely, O LORD. . . . Where can I go from your Spirit? Where can I flee from your presence? If I go up to the heavens, you are there; if I make my bed in the depths, you are there. If I rise on the wings of the dawn, if I settle on the far side of the sea, even there your hand will guide me, your right hand will hold me fast.[14]

The LORD is near.[15]

For a man's ways are in full view of the LORD, and he examines all his paths.[16]

"Can anyone hide in secret places so that I cannot see him?" declares the LORD. "Do I not fill heaven and earth?"[17]

Your [God's] eyes are open to all the ways of men.[18]

"The very hairs of your head are all numbered. So don't be afraid."[19]

"Surely I [Jesus] am with you always, to the very end of the age."[20]

He [God] is not far from each one of us.[21]

"Never will I [God] leave you; never will I forsake you."[22]

These verses represent but a fraction of the total. Any message repeated so often must be important. And it must be one we will have some difficulty grasping. To believe that God sees, knows, and understands everything about every human being; that He sees us individually, not as a generic group; that He stays closer to each one of us than we can stay to each other; that He sees our actions, hears our words, and knows our thoughts requires faith. At times, it even seems we must simply take His word for it. And we do, but not always. Sometimes we forget. Sometimes we doubt. Sometimes we wish He were not scrutinizing our lives so closely, and then a moment later we fear that He has stopped seeing and hearing us — or worse yet, stopped accepting us as we are, with all our foolishness and weakness.

God really is omnipresent. His omnipresence, of course, applies to *all* dimensions and realms, to those we live in (four space-time dimensions), to those we can discover (ten space-time dimensions), and to those beyond what we can discover (heaven, hell, etc.).

God, Invisible and Untouchable

While no one could be more attentive to us, more loving, more understanding, more steadfast, and more aware of our innermost being than God, neither could anyone be more invisible and untouchable. The Bible emphasizes that God is Spirit[23] and describes Him as utterly unapproachable — through our five senses.

God's invisibility and intangibility are just as clearly affirmed in the Bible as are any of His other attributes, including His nearness. Jacob adds an important note to his acknowledgment of God's presence: "Surely the LORD is in this place, and I was not aware of it."[24] God explains to Moses: "No one may see me and live."[25]

As Job, Elihu, Eliphaz, Bildad, and Zophar debate, statements about God's invisibility such as these are made:

When he passes me, I cannot see him. When he goes by, I cannot perceive him.[26]

If I go to the east, he is not there; if I go to the west, I do not find him. When he is at work in the north, I do not see him; when he turns to the south, I catch no glimpse of him.[27]

The Almighty is beyond our reach.[28]

Isaiah gives this description of God: "Truly you are a God who hides himself."[29]

Paul refers to God as "the King, eternal, immortal, invisible, the only God,"[30] and "God . . . whom no one has seen or can see."[31]

John the apostle proclaims the following:

No one has ever seen God.[32]

You have never heard his voice nor seen his form.[33]

No one has seen the Father.[34]

These Scriptures teach not only that no human being has ever seen God but also that it is impossible in any earthly situation for us humans to see God in His totality. God is hidden from us in the sense that we cannot make contact with Him through our five senses. This intangibility we do not appreciate. We cannot help but think that the disciples had an easier time knowing Him, believing Him, understanding Him, trusting Him, and loving Him than we do. How often have we heard ourselves or someone else express the wish that God were right here in person, physically present on Earth?

Jesus' longest recorded conversation addresses this very concern (see John 13–17). During His last evening alone with His twelve disciples, the One whom the twelve had finally recognized as "God with us," reminded them,

"I will be with you only a little longer. You will look for me, and just as I told the Jews, so I tell you now: Where I am going, you cannot come."[35]

These words cut right to the heart. The most wondrous, joyous, and hope-giving season in these men's lives—in the lives of any humans anywhere and anytime to date—was the time they spent in Jesus' company, eating, sleeping, talking, walking, laughing, crying, loving, learning, and ministering side by side. Now He said it was over. He was going away, and they could not come with Him.

The disciples, of course, wanted to know where Jesus was going. Jesus replied, "Where I am going, you cannot follow now, but you will follow later."[36] This answer did not satisfy their curiosity or their longings. They wanted to know why they could not go with Him. Surely their years of service with Him qualified them for better treatment. As Peter pleaded, "Lord, why can't I follow you now? I will lay down my life for you."[37] Peter did not understand that no human being, not even such a fervent friend as he, could yet enter the realm Jesus was about to enter.[38] Jesus replied by telling them plainly that He was going to His Father's house, and that one reason for His soon departure and their later arrival was His desire to prepare a special dwelling place in His Father's house for each one of them.[39]

Jesus' explanation helped some, but the disciples' apprehension and grief still held sway. They did not know anything tangible about the house of which Jesus spoke. They had no idea where this house could be found or what the special dwelling places would be like. Worse yet, they were unsure about how they would get there and about how long they would have to wait before reuniting with Him. And how on earth would they get along without Him? Jesus anticipated their concerns with these words:

> "Because I have said these things, you are filled with grief. But I tell you the truth: It is for your good that I am going away. Unless I go away, the Counselor will not come to you; but if I go, I will send him to you."[40]

The disciples heard His promise: He definitely would not abandon them and leave them to their own resources. But they still did not understand. From their perspective, Jesus answered one mystery with another. While they were puzzling over this second mystery,

Jesus presented them with a third. He told them what they were about to experience would be something like giving birth:

> "You will grieve, but your grief will turn to joy. A woman giving birth to a child has pain because her time has come; but when her baby is born she forgets the anguish because of her joy that a child is born into the world. So with you: Now is your time of grief, but I will see you again and you will rejoice."[41]

With this analogy, Jesus prepared them for great pain and anguish with a promise that this suffering would later seem very brief and completely worthwhile. The joy and help they were about to receive would heal their pain and enable them to cope with His physical departure. And they would be carried along by an increasingly confident hope of reunion with Him, not in familiar surroundings, but in better ones.

The Dimensional Barrier

Accepting the benefits of that departure was not easy for them, especially at first,[42] and it still presents difficulties for us. But we can receive (for the asking), as those who knew Jesus face to face did, both the joy and help of His indwelling Spirit, who will always remain. The awesome benefits of His internal "nearness" will be discussed in a later chapter. What we can begin to address here, through an exercise of our imagination, is the benefit of His physical "distance," which in His case makes possible greater nearness, greater intimacy, than we may have understood was possible.

We can picture in our mind's eye the kind of relationship we could develop with some characters we design on a computer screen. These screen people occupy only the two dimensions of the computer's screen, while we reside in three. Given the right software, we could give them color and animation, and we could create splendid scenes for them to move around in, all the while sending electronic signals to let them know of our presence. In reality, of course, these two-dimensional beings would not possess the capacity to "know" anything because a brain, or nerve center, requires three-dimensionality. But, for the sake of the analogy, we can pretend they are able to think.

As their designers, we know everything about them. Whatever capacities they possess, we gave them. If we enable them to move about the screen, we know the possibilities and the limits of their mobility. Whether they come to recognize the fact or not, their existence depends entirely on us. They have no control over the power supply, the "on" switch, that keeps electricity flowing into the system that is their universe.

Figure 8.1: A Three-Dimensional Being in Proximity to the Screen People
Mr. and Mrs. Screen are two-dimensional beings confined to the plane of length and width on a computer screen. A three-dimensional being can approach their plane from the depth dimension and place a fingertip a hundredth of a millimeter from the body of either one of them. Despite this close proximity, the Screens would be unable to detect the fingertip's presence, much less understand and describe its physical characteristics.

We can imagine the difficulty these screen people would have in comprehending us and relating to us (see figure 8.1). Could they be certain of our existence? Perhaps reasonably so, if they came to recognize their incapacity to create themselves or anything else in their screen environment, and if they discern that their power source is located outside their realm. Could they perceive our three-dimensionality and how it compares with their two-dimensionality? Given adequate research, they may discover enough about themselves and their environment to recognize that a third dimension must exist for them to exist, but they will never fully comprehend what a difference that third dimension makes, nor will they be able to visualize more than two dimensions at a time. Visiting them in person (screen-person, that is) would bridge the gap; but who, then, would stay outside the screen to handle the controls? For us, this is not an option.

As close as these characters may come to each other on the screen, they will remain unable to detect certain things about themselves, characteristics that we can easily observe from our three-dimensional perspective. Because we experience depth, we can stand back from them and instantly see their complete outline or shape. All they can perceive of one another are various lines. If they are round, they may figure out that their bodies are circular by carefully moving around one another, but they will not see each other's circles as we who look on from outside the screen see them. We can program them to rebound off each other and to make a certain sound when they do, but they have only growing or shrinking lines to indicate movement.

Even if we put our hands or faces right up to the screen, perhaps covering them up completely, they cannot see or hear or feel our nearness through the glass barrier. Sending strong vibrations through the glass might only confuse or frighten them—given, of course, that we have endowed them with emotions as well as sense receptors and minds.

We observe something else about the screen people that they can never see. We can see what is inside them. The details and workings of their interior body parts, for example, are fully exposed to us. The amount of information we have about them is at least an order of magnitude (that is, at least a factor of ten times) greater than what any of them possesses.

In this simple analogy, just one dimension separates the screen people from us humans. And yet, the advantage of that one extra dimension suffices to explain how we could be closer to the screen people than they are to each other, fully comprehending them inside and out, while remaining invisible and untouchable to them. Knowing the value of seeing and touching, we could give them the capacity to detect and contact each other, but they would be unable to understand how much more limited these senses are for them than they are for us. They can only detect and contact outer edges, whereas we can see and electronically "touch" every part of them.

God's dimensional advantage over us goes far beyond this one-dimensional difference. He can operate in at least the eleven dimensions established by the string theory (see chapter 3)—and probably many more. His capacity to maintain close and comprehensive contact with us—despite our incapacity to experience Him physically through our space-bound dimensions—becomes a comprehensible reality. We cannot begin to picture it, except perhaps by analogy, but it does make sense.

Making sense of His nearness is more important, for now, than physically sensing His nearness. Pleasure is something our senses can give us, and it is temporary; but joy comes from a source beyond the senses, and it lasts. It comes from discovering and grasping truth, among other things. Pleasure and physical nearness are good, but the pleasures and nearness available to us in His extra dimensions go immeasurably beyond what we can think or imagine, as His written Word declares. In one sense, God's invisibility and untouchability keep our yearnings focused where they rightly belong, on the supernatural realm that awaits us. His written Word combines with evidences in this spectacular but limited physical realm to communicate that His desire and plan involve transporting us, at some future moment along our time line, across our dimensional barriers into His super-dimensional realm.

Below are just a few of the verses in which He expresses His knowability, the benefits of embracing Him through faith, that extra "sense" He has given us. Faith, as defined in Scripture,[43] integrates all the information and evidences we accumulate in our pursuit of truth, and faith takes us beyond mental acceptance of facts to "belief in action," to trust.

If you seek him, he will be found by you.[44]

Come near to God and he will come near to you.[45]

The LORD is near to all who call on him, to all who call on him in truth.[46]

The LORD is close to the brokenhearted.[47]

I [the Lord] live in a high and holy place, but also with him who is contrite and lowly in spirit.[48]

Anyone who comes to him [God] must believe that he exists and that he rewards those who earnestly seek him.[49]

This last verse appears to state necessary conditions for finding Him—believing in His existence and in His desire to reward our search for Him. Another way to look at this verse is to focus on the promise it holds. This promise is that an earnest search for Him will always be rewarded and never disappointed.

These verses and our research into every aspect of God's creation, including the creation's miraculous, extra-dimensional origin, point to a God who wants to be found, to be known, and to be near, not just in the limited ways possible here and now—as essential and wonderful as they are—but in the imagination-stretching ways our three-dimensional, time-bound bodies cannot experience or even survive.

That future crossover into the resurrected, ascended Christ's tangible presence and into His new creation will require some radical alterations in our physical being. Both the Bible and science tell us that these mortal bodies must first be transformed. After all, our bodies are meticulously designed to function in this particular four-dimensional universe with its particular thermodynamics, electromagnetism, and gravity.

Flesh and blood cannot inherit the kingdom of God, nor does the perishable inherit the imperishable.[50]

In a flash . . . the dead will be raised imperishable, and we will be changed. For the perishable must clothe itself with the imperishable, and the mortal with immortality.[51]

The body that is sown is perishable, it is raised imperishable; it is sown in dishonor, it is raised in glory; it is sown in weakness, it is raised in power; it is sown a natural body, it is raised a spiritual body.[52]

These verses suggest we will still have "bodies," individual identities, in the realm to which we are headed, but these bodies will no longer experience fatigue, disease, or decay. Clearly, the laws governing their operation will be different from the laws governing our operation today. Our new bodies will be suited to our new environment. Imagine the screen people's two-dimensional bodies trying to support the screen people anywhere but on the computer monitor's surface. Such bodies would simply be too unstable, too limited and limiting. The same could be said of our present bodies in whatever dimensional realm He intends to place us.

In the words of the apostle John,

Dear friends, now we are children of God, and what we will be has not yet been made known. But we know that when he appears, we shall be like him, for we shall see him as he is.[53]

As we will describe more fully in chapter 17, when we see Him with our own eyes, we will be seeing Him with a new and indescribable sight capacity. All our other capacities will be new, too. In fact, they will be capacities like His, capacities beyond our comprehension, capacities that enable us to participate fully in what He describes as "married life" at home with Him.

CHAPTER NINE

EXTRA-DIMENSIONALITY
AND GOD'S TRIUNITY

One distinctive, extra-dimensional doctrine of the Christian faith is God's triunity. This doctrinal cornerstone, which we can neither adequately picture nor explain, has proved a stumbling block throughout the ages to many people's belief in the God of the Bible.

Jews reject God's triunity or the Trinity as a violation of God's oneness. Muslims mock its "mathematical absurdity" as proof that their beliefs make much more sense than do those of Christians. Cults have emerged around various four-dimensional redefinitions of it. America's famed orator, Daniel Webster, received public ridicule for his acceptance of it: "How can a man of your mental caliber believe that three equals one?"[1]

Biblical Statements on the Trinity

More than five hundred Scripture verses, Old and New Testament, refer to God as both singular and plural (see table 9.1, page 82). Genesis opens with a reference to God the Creator and God the Spirit. When the narrative zooms in on the creation of humans, the writer assigns both singular and plural pronouns to God: "Let us make man in our image, in our likeness."[2] "So God created man in his own image."[3] Several other Bible verses refer to God with both singular and plural pronouns.[4]

One of God's names in Scripture, *Elohim*, is the Hebrew plural form of *El*, the word for God, or god, in the widest possible sense.[5] *Elohim* used as a plural in Scripture can denote pagan images and the imaginary (or demonic) deities they represent (Deuteronomy

4:28 and 12:2). Yet in verses such as Genesis 1:1, the plural form denotes the singular supreme deity.[5-6]

The Bible declares emphatically there is only one Savior,[7] one Creator,[8] one Redeemer,[9] and one Resurrectionist,[10] and yet it identifies two or three members of the Godhead as that one Savior,[11] Redeemer,[11] Creator,[12] and Resurrectionist.[13] The one name God assigns to Himself is the unpronounceable *YHWH*. In one paragraph of Scripture, both God the Father and God the Son lay claim to this name.[14]

When Jesus commissions His disciples for ministry, He instructs them to baptize new believers "in the name of the Father and of the Son and of the Holy Spirit."[15] One name somehow identifies the one and the three. Many other passages imply that our salvation rests on the deity of God the Father, God the Son, and God the Holy Spirit—together, in some unfathomable way, the one and only God.

The charge that "Trinitarians" accept a mathematical absurdity would seem appropriate in light of these and other verses—if the biblical God were confined to the same dimensional realm as humans. Fortunately, He has shown us abundant evidence that He is not. Unfortunately, many of the illustrations Christians use to explain the Trinity are only three-dimensional and may serve to muddy the water more than to clarify it.

Table 9.1: Bible Verses Expounding God's Triunity

Gen. 1:1-3, 26-27	Psalm 139:7-10	Hosea 12:3-5
Gen. 3:22	Prov. 30:2-4	Micah 5:2-5
Gen. 11:7,9	Is. 6:8	Zech. 6:12-13
Gen. 16:7-13	Is. 7:14	Matt. 3:16-17
Gen. 18:1-32	Is. 9:6-7	Matt. 11:27
Gen. 22:11-16	Is. 37:20	Matt. 12:28
Ex. 23:20-23	Is. 41:4	Matt. 22:41-46
Deut. 4:35,39	Is. 43:10-11	Matt. 28:18-20
Deut. 5:7-11	Is. 44:6-8	Mark 1:10-11
Deut. 6:4,13	Is. 45:5,14	Luke 1:35
Deut. 32:39	Is. 45:21-23	Luke 3:21-22
2 Sam. 22:32	Is. 46:9	Luke 10:22
Neh. 9:6	Is. 48:12-17	John 1:1-3,32-34
Job 33:4	Is. 59:15-20	John 5:17-23,37
Psalm 2:2-12	Is. 61:1-3	John 6:27
Psalm 110	Jer. 23:5-6	John 8:58

John 10:17-18,30-39	2 Cor. 13:14	Heb. 1:1-8
John 14:6-11,16-26	Gal. 1:3	Heb. 9:14
John 15:26	Gal. 3:20,26	James 2:19
John 16:7-15	Eph. 1:2,13-14,17	1 Peter 1:2
John 17:1-11, 21-24	Eph. 4:3-6	1 Peter 2:4
John 20:28	Phil. 1:2	1 Peter 3:18
Acts 2:30-36	Phil. 2:5-11	1 Peter 4:14
Acts 5:3-4	Col. 1:15-17	2 Peter 1:1-2,16-17
Acts 17:29-30	Col. 2:9-10	1 John 1:2-3
Acts 20:28	1 Thess. 1:1-5	1 John 4:2-3
Rom. 1:4,7	2 Thess. 1:2	1 John 4:9-15
Rom. 3:30	2 Thess. 2:13-17	2 John 3-4,9
Rom. 8:9-11,26-29	1 Tim. 1:2,17	Jude 1-4,20-21,25
Rom. 9:1-5	1 Tim. 2:5	Rev. 1:1,4-5
Rom. 16:25-27	1 Tim. 6:13-16	Rev. 2:27-29
1 Cor. 1:3	2 Tim. 3:15–4:1	Rev. 4:8-11
1 Cor. 2:10-16	Titus 1:2-4	Rev. 5:2-7,12-13
1 Cor. 8:4-6	Titus 2:11-14	Rev. 6:16-17
1 Cor. 12:3-6	Titus 3:4-6	Rev. 15:3-8
2 Cor. 1:2,21-22	Phlm. 3	Rev. 19:15-16

One popular illustration compares the Trinity to an individual's simultaneous multiple identity as, for example, a father, a son, and a grandson. In this illustration we have one being with three different relationship labels that can be applied simultaneously. But we do not have three persons who are capable of relating to one another in any self-distinctive way.

Another illustration likens the Trinity to water at its "triple point" (32° F or 0° C), the temperature at which it can be ice or liquid or vapor. Water can take all three forms and still retain its distinctive molecular makeup, but any particular quantity of water will typically take one form and not the others. Or some fraction of it will take one form, say liquid, while another fraction takes another form, say ice, and perhaps another fraction, the other form, vapor. It cannot be 100 percent liquid, 100 percent ice, and 100 percent steam at the same time.

The sun provides another familiar illustration of oneness and threeness—the sun is simultaneously a star, a light source, and a heat source. We see the sun's light and feel its heat without having tangible contact with the sun. The light and heat manifest to us the sun's properties, as God manifests His properties through the Son and the Holy Spirit. This illustration seems helpful at first glance, but it falters on two important points. First, the sun's heat is not an individual entity in any way but rather a portion of the sun's light spectrum. Second, the light and heat energy coming from the sun cannot be considered from any perspective as equivalent to the sun itself.

Some Bible scholars have proposed the picture of a cake, which simultaneously can be thought of as ingredients, layers, and slices. The ingredients would represent the Father; the layers, the Son; and the slices, the Holy Spirit distributed to individual believers. To paraphrase a cliché, the problem here is that we cannot have a cake and eat its pieces, too. Once the slices are all distributed or eaten, neither the layers nor the cake would remain intact.

Another illustration uses light, heat, and air to represent the Trinity.[16] Each has its individual properties and obeys different sets of physical laws, yet all three are essential to life. This illustration shares a weakness with the sun analogy. Heat is but a subset of light. It also falls short in reflecting the Trinity's oneness, for light (including heat) and air have totally distinct properties.

Benjamin B. Warfield's favorite analogy for the Trinity is the human being, the express "image of God."[17] Humans are body, soul, and spirit, the three performing distinct functions yet unified, as may be said of the Trinity. One drawback to this illustration is its cultural and theological bias. Only some cultural, philosophical, and theological systems make a distinction between soul and spirit. Perhaps a more serious problem is the difference in limitations among these three aspects of a person. The body cannot live apart from the soul and spirit, but the soul and spirit do continue to exist when the body dies.

One significant weakness hampers each of these (and many other) thought-provoking Trinity illustrations. They attempt to explain a supernatural, extra-dimensional being in the frame of reference we four-dimensional beings occupy. Thus, well-meaning as their originators are, each illustration is doomed to reflect some distortion of God's identity—distortions or partial truths often characterizing cults and other religious systems. One distortion portrays the Trinity as a plurality, characteristic of polytheistic systems: God is a divine triumvirate in total agreement to work cooperatively toward one purpose. Another distortion, built in defense of monotheism, presents a modalistic entity: a personal Being who manifests Himself in one of three different modes—Father, Son, or Spirit—at different times and in different circumstances as He sees fit. Neither of these views aligns with biblical revelation. Indeed, they cannot. All naturalistic, four-dimensional representations of the Trinity must reflect either tritheism or modalism. Our human frame of reference holds no other options.

Creedal Statements of the Trinity Doctrine

The early church fathers, recognizing the importance of nipping heresies and cults in the bud, took painstaking care to explain in what sense God is plural and in what sense singular. They accomplished this task by convening councils to write creeds. Because few people of their time had access to education, even to basic literacy, these scholars labored to prepare accurate, brief, and easy-to-memorize statements of the faith. The most famous of such creeds expounding the doctrines of Christianity is the Nicene Creed, penned in the fourth century A.D. The following excerpt focuses on the Trinity:

> I believe in one God, the Father Almighty, Maker of heaven and earth, and of all things visible and invisible.
> And I believe in one Lord, Jesus Christ, the only-begotten Son of God, born of the Father before all ages. God of God, Light of Light, true God of true God; begotten, not made, of one substance with the Father. By whom all things are made. . . .
> And I believe in the Holy Spirit, the Lord and Giver of life, who proceeds from the Father and the Son. Who together with the Father and the Son is adored and glorified.

The Nicene Creed, while declaring there is but one God, specifically assigns deity to the Father, the Son, and the Holy Spirit. Each is declared to be the Creator. Their oneness is explained in terms of their being of "one substance."

The Athanasian Creed, developed in the same era, focused more on defending the doctrine of Christ's deity, a significant aspect of the Trinity doctrine but with a narrower focus.

Reformation Confessions of the Trinity

With the dawning of the Reformation and the spread of literacy, Bible scholars saw the need for more detailed written explanations of the Trinity. Two great confessions of the Christian faith were published. A committee of German Lutheran theologians prepared the first of these, entitled "A Confession of Faith," presented to Germany's King Charles V in Augsburg in 1530. The second came from the Assembly of the Divines, a consortium of Anglican theologians commissioned by the British House of Commons and House of Lords. This group devoted five years to the writing of the Westminster Confession, adopted by the British parliament and the Churches of England and Scotland in 1648.

Both the Augsburg and Westminster Confessions are lengthy documents, but their statements on the Trinity are relatively brief. Article One of the Augsburg Confession reads as follows:

> Our churches teach with great unanimity that the decree of the Council of Nicaea concerning the unity of the divine essence and concerning the three persons is true and should be believed without any doubting. That is to say, there is one divine essence, which is called and which is God, eternal, incorporeal, indivisible, of infinite power, wisdom, and goodness, the maker and preserver of all things, visible and invisible. Yet there are three persons, of the same essence and power, who are also coeternal: the Father, the Son, and the Holy Spirit. And the term "person" is used, as the ancient Fathers employed it in this connection, to signify not a part or a quality in another but that which subsists of itself.
>
> Our churches condemn all heresies that have sprung up against this article, such as that of the Manichaeans who posited two principles, one good and the other evil, and also those of the Valentinians, Arians, Eunomians,

Mohammedans, and all others like these. They also condemn the Samosatenes, old and new, who contend that there is only one person and craftily and impiously argue that the Word and the Holy Spirit are not distinct persons since "Word" signifies a spoken word and "Spirit" signifies a movement that is produced in things.[18]

The Westminster Confession, chapter 2, article 3, makes the following declaration:

In the unity of the Godhead there be three persons, of one substance, power, and eternity; God the Father, God the Son, and God the Holy Ghost. The Father is of none, neither begotten nor proceeding; the Son is eternally begotten of the Father; the Holy Ghost eternally proceeding from the Father and the Son.[19]

The Augsburg Confession adds to the Nicene Creed an attempt to clarify what the word "Persons" means and does not mean with respect to the Godhead. This treatise specifies that each member of the Trinity exists or "subsists" on His own and is more than merely a part of the existence of the other members. To put it another way, the Augsburg Confession emphasizes that the divine Persons are not mere aspects or portions of God's Being, but are distinct, personal Entities who nonetheless manifest the unity of the divine Being.

The Westminster Confession declares the unity of the Godhead with full recognition of the three personal distinctions included within the Godhead. The confession also explains at length what God's eternality implies for each member of the Godhead in His dealings with individual human beings.

Lutherans quickly and universally adopted the Augsburg Confession, as did Anglicans the Westminster Confession. In fact, the scholarly excellence of these works still stands. Most Protestant, evangelical denominations and independent congregations have incorporated one or both in their own statements of faith.[20-21]

Modern Formulations of the Trinity

Some of the twentieth century's most distinguished Bible scholars have devoted themselves to updating the language of the church's doctrinal statements. They acknowledge that current culture demands not only more familiar vocabulary and syntax but also a return to brevity. James M. Boice offers the following summations:

1. There is but one living and true God who exists in three persons: God the Father, God the Son, and God the Holy Spirit.
2. The Lord Jesus Christ is fully divine, being the second person of the Godhead, who became man.
3. The Holy Spirit is fully divine.
4. While each is fully divine, the three persons of the Godhead are related to each other in a way that implies some differences.
5. In the work of God the members of the Godhead work together.[22]

Boice adds that the knowledge, feelings, and will of each person within the Godhead—Father, Son, and Holy Spirit—are identical.[23]

Charles C. Ryrie condenses the Trinity doctrine into this brief declaration:

There is one only and true God, but in the unity of the Godhead there are three eternal and coequal Persons, the same in substance and distinct in subsistence.[24]

Ryrie borrows the word *subsistence* from John Calvin to distinguish independent "sustenance" from "independent personalities," a confusion sometimes arising from the use of the word *Persons*.

Geoffrey Bromiley states the doctrine this way:

Within the one essence of the Godhead we have to distinguish three "persons" who are neither three gods on the one side, nor three parts or modes of God on the other, but coequally and coeternally God.[25]

Recognizing that "essence" and "persons" are inadequate terms for the Trinity, Bromiley's statement seeks to distinguish what the orthodox Christian scholars imply and do not imply about the application of these terms to God.[26]

R. A. Finlayson offers these operational definitions of the Godhead:

+ The Trinity expresses unity in diversity. There are not three individuals, but three personal self-distinctions. . . . Each person is self-conscious and self-directing, yet never acting independently [that is, expressing independence of will, actions, or feelings].
+ The Trinity expresses equality in dignity. All three Persons of the Trinity are perfectly equal in nature, honor, and dignity.
+ The Trinity expresses diversity in operation. Each Person of the Godhead performs different functions that involve certain degrees of subordination (in relation, though not in nature).[27]

Finlayson describes how the nature, operation, and expression of the Trinity enable God to reveal Himself to humans and commune with them. He explains how the Trinity provides for humanity's redemption and for all true fellowship among His spirit creatures.[28]

One immeasurable value of all these doctrinal creeds, confessions, and statements lies in their uncompromising preservation of the paradoxical nature of the Trinity. They present a doctrine that can be true only in a realm beyond what we humans experience.

Illustrating the Trinity's Extra-Dimensionality

Given that our attempts to illustrate the Trinity may distort and damage people's understanding of God more than they help, we may feel inclined to abandon all attempts at illustration and stick solely to our creeds and confessions. But this abandonment poses an equally serious risk: the loss of an important communication tool—and more.

For Christians to offer only the hard-to-comprehend and abstract words of our creeds, doctrines, and confessions suggests to many people that God is distant and incomprehensible—perhaps merely a reflection of humanity's weaknesses, fears, and larger-than-life imagination. Though we know God cannot be understood completely by human beings, He does give ample evidence that He desires to be known and is knowable.

What may prove most helpful to believers and unbelievers alike would be the development of illustrations of the Trinity that cross the dimensional limitations of human experience without doing undue damage to biblical definitions and doctrine. Better yet, we may simply find ways to portray the difficulties we four-dimensional creatures face in our attempts to comprehend our super-dimensional God. The difficulty, of course, lies in our inability to visualize phenomena in a realm beyond our experience. In other words, an illustration involving more than our familiar four dimensions will cease to illustrate.

A   B

Figure 9.1: Screen People's Perception of a 3-D Hand Near Their Plane
Looking edge-on to the screen people's plane, **A**, the hand, though close to the plane, makes no contact with it. Looking straight on to the plane, view **B**, no part of the hand is present on the plane, and, therefore, the hand is invisible to the screen people.

So, what illustrative options do we have? One that comes to mind involves a crossover from the four dimensions we experience to a realm with fewer dimensions. Such an illustration, while not completely analogous, may help us make some sense of our struggle to understand how God can possibly be one and three at the same time without violating the rules of logic and reason, including basic arithmetic.

Figure 9.2: Screen People's Perception of a Fingertip of the 3-D Hand Just Touching or Grazing Their Plane
Looking edge-on to the screen people's plane, **A**, a fingertip of the 3-D hand barely makes contact with the plane. In the plane itself, **B**, the hand shows up only as a single point, a point that would disappear and reappear as the fingertip is pushed into and away from the screen.

Let us revisit the illustration of the computer screen people presented in chapter 8. We can try to imagine (and this calls for plenty of imagination!) what would happen if we brought one of our three-dimensional hands into contact with the two-dimensional computer screen people. Remember, since our hand exists in a third dimension perpendicular to the plane of the screen people, its position outside the screen will always be defined by them as "above" or "below" them, though we see its position as "beside" the screen.

Now, as long as our hand remains above the plane of the screen people, they cannot observe or detect anything at all about our existence, our characteristics, our powers, or our modes of operation (see figure 9.1, page 90). If we were to touch their plane with the very tip of one finger, however, they would see us as a single point, a point that can, as the finger touches and withdraws from the plane, appear and disappear at any time (see figure 9.2, page 91). If we were to touch their plane with the bottom side of an extended finger, they would see us as a line (see figure 9.3). If instead of a finger extended straight out, we were to touch their plane with the bottom side of a curled up finger, they would see us as a curved line.

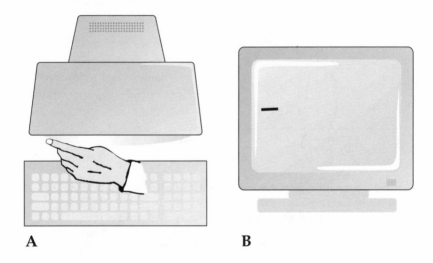

A   **B**

Figure 9.3: Screen People's Perception of the Side of an Extended Finger of a 3-D Hand Just Touching Their Plane
With the side of an extended finger of the 3-D hand just touching the screen people's plane, **A**, the screen people observe it as, **B**, a single short line. If that finger is curled a little, the screen people would see the hand transform from a straight line into a curved line.

If the screen were not a solid barrier to us, we could push a finger vertically (that is, perpendicularly) into their plane (see figure 9.4, page 93). This time the screen people would see us as a small, slightly irregular circle. If we were to push it deeper, they would observe us as an enlarging irregular circle. If instead of penetrating their plane with one finger exactly perpendicular to their plane we were to penetrate it at some other angle to their plane (see figure 9.5, page 94), they would now behold us as an elongated ellipse, which could enlarge depending on the degree of penetration.

A   B

Figure 9.4: Screen People's Perception of a Finger of a 3-D Hand Poking Through Their Plane
With the finger penetrating their plane, **A**, the screen people now see the 3-D hand as a small circle, **B**. As the finger pokes through the plane farther, the screen people would see first the fingertip, then, eventually, a cross-section of the first knuckle of the finger. The finger would appear to them to transform from a point into progressively larger circles.

From the screen people's perspective, the finger could appear at different times as a point, a straight line, a curved or angled line, a small irregular circle, a larger irregular circle, an elongated ellipse of variable size, or not even appear at all. They could easily conclude that the same finger is six or more different entities, each manifesting some distinct characteristics. They might never discern that the six-plus manifestations were all governed by one entity and one source of operation.

A   **B**

Figure 9.5: Screen People's Perception of a Finger of a 3-D Hand Penetrating Their Plane at a Non-Perpendicular Angle
With the finger poking through their plane at any angle other than perpendicular, **A**, the screen people see the 3-D hand as an elongated ellipse, **B**.

The analogy illustrates at least to some degree how we can misunderstand God's contact with our world. Because He manifests Himself to the human race at different times and in different ways, we may conclude that God is not one but several deities or that He is one totally changeable, unpredictable, and undefinable deity. Consider people's confusion over Christ's manifestations of Himself as the Creator, as the Angel of the Lord, as Jesus of Nazareth, as the sacrificial Lamb of God, as Judge, and as much more. Some sects, for instance, insist that the angel of the Lord cannot be Christ. Others refuse to acknowledge Christ's authority and action as either the Creator or the Judge.

Let us take this illustration of the screen people and the human hand further. Instead of penetrating the plane of the screen people with just one finger, we could penetrate it with two, three, or more fingers, and each of these would enter at a slightly different angle from the others. We could bend our pointer finger so that the fingertip just touches, making a small dot, while our thumb passes into the plane sideways, making an elongated ellipse, and our middle finger passes straight through the plane perpendicularly, making an irregular circle. If we move these fingers, they may appear to the screen people to be functioning in complete independence of each other.

In this extension of the illustration, the screen people would be tempted to conclude that this higher being contacting their realm might be three different and independently operating beings. They would see the hand as at least something like themselves, a number of independently functioning, closed line segments. In fact, from the screen people's perspective, these closed surfaces (each circle or ellipse closes off a specific area) could not possibly constitute one closed surface, for the screen people would be unable to see how closed surfaces could be anything other than closed line segments.

In three spatial dimensions, however, the fingers and thumb belong to the single closed surface that encompasses our body. What the screen people could not see, nor even comprehend, is how the various circles and ellipses can be united into the surface, that is, the skin, that encloses a body (or even a part of it, the hand). Though they see segments of the fingers, they would not be able to visualize the totality of the fingers, and they would have no concept of the hand. The twoness, threeness, or moreness of our hand (or one aspect of that plurality) they could imagine, but not the oneness. In fact, their concept of our hand's oneness would be so unfathomable as to appear impossible and thus "incorrect."

The reverse difficulty could just as easily occur. If we were to pass our outstretched hand, fingers and thumb pressed tightly together, through the plane right up to the wrist, the screen people would attest to the oneness of our hand while remaining ignorant of, and perhaps arguing against, the plurality manifest by our separate fingers.

Screen People Theologians
In response to the revelation of various cross-sections of our fingers, one group of screen people might become the equivalent of convinced polytheists, certain that multiple higher beings exist who can never be treated in any context as one. In response to the revelation of the wrist cross-section, another group of screen people

might become the equivalent of a category of monotheists who insist that the one higher being can never, in any context, be two or more. We can also imagine both groups decrying the absurdity of a simultaneous plural and singular higher being.

Taking the illustration still further, we can imagine a plethora of debates among screen people who saw dots, lines (of different configurations), circles and ellipses (of different sizes), staying still or moving, appearing or disappearing, enlarging or shrinking. At some point, one group might band together to found the Church of the Three Circles, while another group launches the Ellipsoid Society, another the Two Circle Fellowship, another the Science of Lines, and yet another the Church of the One True Ellipse. These groups might divide up through time, of course, and new groups begin as new interpretations of the revelations arise.

The teachings of each group might be similar in some points, but for the most part sharply divergent. We can imagine the ensuing conflicts that might arise should attempts be made to overlook differences and to unite against big social problems. We can even imagine the cynicism of some screen people who say all this talk of higher beings means nothing; all that has appeared is some amazing but explicable (with enough research) screen phenomenon that, once understood, will usher in a new age of screen people consciousness.

The great irony of the disagreement about the higher being is that none of these groups and individuals has more than a tiny clue about who that being is and what that being can do. All have an incredibly limited perspective on the attributes of the being, especially on the powers available to him or her.

What if one bold group of the screen people dared to acknowledge both the plural and singular manifestations of the higher being as possibly connected? Some of the screen people may have studied our contacts closely enough to watch our fingers enter their plane from above and continue to move down through their plane until the fingers converged in a cross-section of our palm (see figure 9.6, page 97). These screen people would see that we first appeared as dots, but then the dots enlarged to form slightly irregular circles, which then flared on one or two sides and eventually merged into one elongated sausage shape (see figure 9.7, page 98). The flares for each of the circles would become larger and eventually join together. This group of screen people might try to tell the others that the plurality somehow became a singularity.

If this group drew its conclusions too quickly, without waiting to see us withdraw our hand so that the shapes change from sausage back to circles back to dots, they might conclude that what was once four has become one and is no longer four.

We can imagine what would be possible if some members of this screen group had received and read some electronic code from the person to whom the hand belongs. Based on their confidence that the code came from outside and spoke of possibilities beyond their screen life, this group might be willing to accept what they cannot picture, that a three-dimensional being does exist and can exist as a fourness and oneness simultaneously, continuously, and permanently. They could, then, draw up a Quadrinity doctrinal statement.

A **B**

Figure 9.6: Screen People's Perception of Four Fingers of a 3-D Hand Poking Through Their Plane
With four fingers of the 3-D hand penetrating their plane, **A**, the screen people now see the hand as four slightly irregular circles, **B**. As the fingers enter the plane, the screen people would see first a point, which grows into a small circle just as another point appears and begins to grow into a circle, then another and another till they see four slightly irregular circles.

They could affirm through review of their observations that the fourness they saw did not negate the oneness of the hand (though they would not really understand that word), nor did the oneness negate the fourness. Realizing they could observe only two of the hand's dimensions at a time but that the hand must exist in a higher realm, they could conclude that the revealed oneness neither detracts from nor contradicts the fourness and that the fourness neither detracts from nor contradicts the oneness. They would never, as part of the screen world, be able to picture these truths. But with some trust in the motivation of the higher being to make contact and explain him or herself truthfully (say through electronic messages), and perhaps by combining their observations with some research in higher-dimensional math problems, these screen people could determine the validity of their conclusions about the hand and the limited validity or downright invalidity of others' conclusions.

A   **B**

Figure 9.7: Screen People's Perception of Four Fingers of a 3-D Hand Penetrating Their Plane Almost up to the Palm
With the four fingers poking through the screen's plane almost up to the palm, **A**, the screen people would see the middle circles develop flares on two sides, moving toward one-sided flares from the outside circles, **B**. As the hand penetrates beyond the fingers and down to the palm, the screen people would observe the flaring circles fusing together to become one larger sausage-shaped object.

Even this group of screen people would possess, at best, an extremely limited view of the nature and capacities of the three-dimensional hand. Their view of the higher being would acknowledge significantly more, but nowhere near *all* of the hand's (or the whole higher being's) power and capability than do the other screen people, the mistaken ones. But the Quadrinitarians' view of the hand's potential still falls enormously short of the hand's—and the whole higher being's—actual potential.

What we must not overlook in this screen people illustration is that the dimensional difference between the screen people and ourselves, the "higher beings" in the analogy, adds up to just one. If we endow them, imaginatively, with enough resources, they could calculate some of the possibilities, capacities, and characteristics of our extra dimension and by how much these exceed the limits of their two dimensions. Though such understanding would give them a genuine basis for awe and wonder, it would still fall far short of reality. Perhaps it would motivate them to ask the higher being for further assistance in believing and knowing what the hand can do.

Limits of the Extra-Dimensional Illustrations

While the analogy of the hand in two and three spatial dimensions is more useful than the others for the Trinity, it is still not complete. Ultimately, the hand is bound to a set number of dimensions of space. God is not. Whereas the fingers are not individually the hand but only aspects of it, Jesus Christ is, for example, fully God.

A more accurate, but still inadequate, illustration could be developed if we were to create an analogy in which we three-dimensional beings interact with individuals confined to only one dimension of space—linelanders, as opposed to the screen people. And, further, what we have illustrated with extra space dimensions should also be illustrated with extra time dimensions.

Even the best extra-dimensional analogies we humans could develop for God's triunity will fall short. We do not know the extent of God's attributes, capacities, and extra-dimensionality. Though we certainly can expose more of God's threeness and oneness to human comprehension, ultimately there are limits to what we can discover.

The intent of this analogy of our hand visiting screenland is to stimulate our thinking about God's powers and attributes, including His triunity, from an extra-dimensional perspective. With the creativity God has given us, we can surely develop more and better analogies with which to build our own faith and spark the faith of others.

One important gap in our understanding and depiction of the Trinity has to do with the interrelationship of God's will and emotions. All of the modern formulations of Trinity doctrine emphasize that the three Persons within the Godhead never respond with independent decisions, desires, or actions. Though the Bible affirms that all of God's responses end up in total unity, the process toward these responses may be more complicated than we can grasp.

Jesus manifests some level of freedom and independence of will if His temptation by Satan in the desert represents anything more than just a formality.[29] At Gethsemane Jesus prays three times, "My Father, if it is possible, may this cup be taken from me. Yet not as I will, but as you will."[30] The Gospels record that Jesus' soul was overwhelmed with sorrow to the point of death, that His emotions were so intense He sweat drops of blood.[31] Obviously, some kind of interaction of the wills takes place between the Son and the Father.

Jesus prays for all of His followers to be one, just as He and the Father are one.[32] He defines this oneness as being a "complete unity."[33]

We see here, at the divine level, a hint of some aspect of the simultaneous operation of free will and predestination, a subject addressed in later chapters. God's unsearched treasures of wisdom and understanding challenge us to keep digging.

Enlarging Our View

How many of us are willing to admit that our view of God soars just slightly above the horizon of our four-dimensional realm? If we laughed at the Quadrinitarians' gross underestimates of the nature, powers, and capacities of the three-dimensional hand, what can we say for ourselves? These hypothetical screen people made their gross underestimates in a realm just one dimension short of the hand's realm. Our human realm falls at least seven and possibly more dimensions (or their equivalent) short of God's realm. This dimensional difference means that our underestimation of God is many geometric orders of magnitude greater than we can imagine even with the help of a dimension-crossing illustration.

This enormous degree of underestimation seems difficult, if not impossible, to grasp. The following numerical analogies may provide some tangibility to the gap we need to bridge.

Without question, the screen people with the most accurate vision of the nature, powers, and capacities of the 3-D hand underestimated its reality by at least a factor of a trillion (the number more likely approaches infinity). Since God possesses at least seven dimensions of advantage over us, rather than just one, we doctrinally orthodox Christians potentially underestimate God's nature, powers, and capacities by at least a factor of a trillion in one dimension, a trillion to the trillionth power in that dimension plus the next dimension (that is, given the existence of two extra dimensions, our underestimation must be a trillion to the trillionth power), and a trillion to the trillionth power to the trillionth power to the trillionth power to the trillionth power to the trillionth power to the trillionth power in seven extra dimensions. In mathematical notation this underestimation factor would be

$$10^{12^{\left(10^{12}\right)^{\left(10^{12}\right)^{\left(10^{12}\right)^{\left(10^{12}\right)^{\left(10^{12}\right)^{\left(10^{12}\right)}}}}}}}$$

Each 10^{12} power (indicated by the superscript) means the number below it must be multiplied by itself some 1,000,000,000,000 times. Given the limitations of our universe, we humans could never even write out this number in standard notation, a one followed by zeros. If all the galaxies in the universe were packed tightly with books full of zeros set in six-point type, the universe could not accommodate the zeros included up to just the third index of this enormous number. But, given that the underestimation factor is more like infinity than it is a mere million, the underestimating factor really would be more like infinity to the infinity power to the infinity power to the infinity power to the infinity power to the infinity power to the infinity power, or in mathematical notation, $\infty^{\infty^{\infty^{\infty^{\infty^{\infty^{\infty^{\infty^{\infty}}}}}}}}$ times.

Sometimes we Christians glibly declare our belief that God is infinitely greater than we can think or imagine, never realizing that the attributions of just a first order infinity (infinity not taken to any power in the index) to God absurdly underestimates Him. We verbally acknowledge His immeasurable power, grace, wisdom, love, and so on, yet our prayers, concerns, actions, and attitudes treat Him as One who is only an order of magnitude (if that) beyond us. The value of mathematically calculating a minimum limit to the superiority of God's powers and capabilities over ours lies in its potential to deliver us from such a tremendous underestimation of God. It should certainly sweep away doubts about God's capacity to manifest Himself as a Triune Being.

And it may add some punch to the apostle Paul's prayer that we will be able, more and more through time, "to grasp how wide and long and high and deep is the love of Christ, and to know this love that surpasses knowledge."[34] A tiny speck of faith placed in His hand can accomplish far more than the relocation of a mountain. It can change our lives profoundly, giving us new courage to face our past, present, and future.

CHAPTER TEN

EXTRA-DIMENSIONALITY, THE INCARNATION, AND THE ATONEMENT

An option unavailable to us in our desire to communicate with the screen people would be to affirm our existence and make our characteristics known face to face. Such an option would be open to us only if we had the capacity to change our dimensionality. But we cannot gain an extra dimension through which to operate. Neither can we put aside a dimension in which we operate. But what if we did have that capacity? What if we could choose to become screen people? Given the costs involved in such a choice, what would motivate us to go through with it?

Far beyond those costs and motivations is the Incarnation. We humans have barely begun to appreciate the gift of the Incarnation in which Jesus chose to divest Himself of not one, but many dimensions or their equivalent. As our appreciation of His choice grows, so will our comprehension of what His love means.

Who Exactly Is the Incarnate Christ?

The Incarnation—coming in the flesh[1]—refers to God's entering human life in a human body. Jesus Christ, the second person of the triune God, the Creator of all angels and of the entire universe, actually became a man. He did this of His own free will, without external compulsion. The Incarnation is possible—God on Earth, God with and among us *and* God in heaven—because of God's extra-dimensional capacities.

Jesus' divine identity as God, His character, wisdom, purity, and motives, remained perfectly intact,[2-3] but He voluntarily relinquished the independent use of His divine attributes and His extra-dimensional capacities. He accepted all the functional limitations of a human brain and body, all the needs, weaknesses, desires, sufferings, and trials of human life apart from sin (or sinning).[4]

Many distinguished theologians have devoted their careers to exploring and expounding the mysteries of the Incarnation, delineating what it means and what it does not mean. For example, some describe how Christ became fully human without inheriting or committing any sin. They cite Scripture passages indicating that He did not inherit His humanity from either Adam or Joseph. Scripture tells us that God supernaturally entered the womb of a virgin (Mary).[5-6] How He interacted with or modified Mary's egg is not made clear in Scripture, but He became a flesh and blood embryo. At that point, Christ received the physical and spiritual aspects of a human being. But as God's Son, He was free, and could be kept free, from the pollution of sin. We have much more to learn from discussions of a doctrine so central to the Christian faith, and I defer to the expertise of biblical expositors.

What we can achieve by an extra-dimensional physics'-eye-view of the Incarnation is a more complete understanding of what Christ willingly endured on behalf of those who would believe His message. And we can gain a new perspective on how He could be at once both God and man, in heaven and on earth, omnipotent and weary, working miracles and praying for miracles, fully God, yet acknowledging God the Father as greater.

Both God and Man

We human beings have no control over the four dimensions we experience; we can neither gain a dimension nor lose one. But God's control and mastery is complete. He created our four dimensions, and several more. Obviously, if God can create and enter dimensions, He can remove and leave them. With such capacities, He has free reign in choosing which ones He will use to interact with us. Further, He can choose to be bound to or use one set of dimensions for certain contexts while choosing other sets of dimensions for other contexts.

Examples of Jesus' control over dimensionality while He was

with us in human form may be found throughout the four Gospels. One appears in the accounts of the temptation by Satan. Jesus, near death from starvation, was reminded of His supernatural capabilities. All Jesus had to do, Satan goaded, was to turn the stones scattered about Him into bread.[7] Such a proposal would pose no temptation for any of us for the simple reason that we would be unable to act on it. The temptation might sharpen our hunger pangs when we heard mention of bread. It might tempt us to hurl some of those stones at our tempter. But to transform the stones into food would be impossible for us. Satan's approach in this temptation suggests that though Jesus had imposed on Himself the limitations common to humanity, He retained the capacity to deliver Himself from those limitations at any time and any place He chose.

A more explicit demonstration of Jesus' total, uninterrupted (but not independent) authority over the dimensions and components of His creation may be seen in the story of the stormy sea of Galilee crossing. While Jesus slept in the stern of the boat, a squall came up, threatening to capsize the vessel. Fearing for their lives, the disciples awakened Jesus. When He saw the men's panic, Jesus at once rebuked the wind and told the waves, "Be still!"[8] Immediately, the wind died down and the surface of the water became completely calm.

This incident shows Jesus' capacity to transition between contexts. First we see Jesus submitting to the wind and waves He created. In the next moment, however, Jesus exercises control and authority, as God the Father's agent, over the elements. In the first context, we see Jesus' humanity. In the second, we see His divinity. Jesus can be both God and man because He alone can choose when and where and with what part of His being and essence to operate in whatever form and over whatever dimensions He pleases.

An Atoning God

God's purpose in the Incarnation goes far beyond breaking through the dimensional barrier to communicate with us face-to-face, to help us understand and believe His message, to show us His love, and to give us hope. He came to break the sin barrier, to repair the damage done in the Garden of Eden. Christ came in human flesh to be the second Adam, the Man who would resist the temptation to "do his own thing." In perfectly obeying the Father, even to the point of death, He would finalize God's victory over the original and most powerful insurrectionist, Satan. The author of Hebrews explains at length why our Redeemer, the mediator between God and humankind, had to share in our humanity,[9] to be made like us in every way,[10] tempted in every way as we are,[11] and yet without any sin.[11-13]

The cornerstone of the Christian faith is the doctrine of the Atonement: We human beings, all born with a propensity to serve ourselves rather than God,[14] what the Bible calls sin, can be "acquitted" because Christ stepped in and paid sin's full penalty. Jesus' perfect life and substitutionary death restores to humanity the possibility of a personal, loving, shameless, never-ending relationship with our Creator. This relationship is available to anyone for the asking—an asking that paradoxically costs us both nothing[15] and everything.[16]

Christ's death to save "whosoever believes in Him"[17] is a doctrine on which Christians generally agree. Disagreements typically arise over other Atonement-related doctrinal issues, such as the meaning of "believe in," the requirements for receiving and keeping God's gift of salvation, and the freedom or pre-determination of our decision to accept that gift. These topics will be discussed in later chapters. For the moment we will focus on other Atonement perplexities: How could God be dead and alive at the same time? Does Christ's death pay for all people's sin or just the sin of those who accept His pardon? How could one man's suffering for several hours cover all the wickedness of all the people who have ever lived or will live?

These questions, among many others, reflect our three-dimensional (plus time) thinking about Christ's Atonement. They cannot be answered self-consistently within the confines of that perspective. But answers can be found if we look beyond our earthly context and consider what is possible in God's extra-dimensional existence.

Simultaneous Death and Life?

When Jesus of Nazareth died on the cross, much more happened than a physical death. The book of Romans reminds us that sin entered the world through one human's decision to disregard God's way and to act on his own authority.[18] This first expression of sin did not cause Adam and Eve to immediately drop dead physically. Physical death came to them some time later.[19] Neither did they lose their capacity to hear God's voice. But sin's consequences were indeed profound. Humanity tasted autonomy, a separation of self from the Source of all life, goodness, truth, and love. The branch disconnected itself from the vine and sought sustenance elsewhere. The evils, pains, and sufferings that followed in Adam and Eve's lives and in the lives of all their progeny demonstrate the devastating results of that initial separation.

Adam and Eve were not the first creatures ever to taste autonomy. But they were the first human beings to taste it, and in doing so they placed themselves, their family, and all their descendants in the camp of God's enemy, the instigator of all insubordination and evil: Satan. Who could repair such damage? Adam was helpless to do so, however remorseful he may have been. No human after him could accomplish the repair, for each was born of that separated branch. The angels, however magnificent and obedient, lacked the capacity to carry it out.[20]

Only God Himself could make the mend. He alone could survive the journey across the gap and make possible the restoration. The Restorer had to be able to enter not just some, but *all* the dimensions and realms occupied by both man and God. Angels could be sent into contact with humanity's dimensions. But the sin gap could not be closed by them, for they could not enter all of man's dimensions and realms and all of God's. Neither did they possess the attributes, resources, and extra-dimensional capacities to pay sin's penalty. One might also point out that the gap was closely guarded by Satan, whom no other angelic being could overpower.

In one moment—for Him, what could be an eternal moment because of His extra dimension(s) of time—Christ crossed the divide caused by sin. The Bible says, "God made him who had no sin to be sin for us,"[21] taking into Himself the wound of separation, the enmity or wrath of God against sin. In a human body, He proved His perfect obedience, His wisdom, and His power to live—and die—with the capacity for autonomy and yet wholly ("holy") attuned to the Father's will. He lived up to God's perfection and qualified Himself to pay the ransom price, namely His own death, for the penalty incurred by humanity's sin.

His death in the physical dimensions of time and space was real, not feigned, an experience He chose to undergo on our behalf. But He also experienced the indescribable spiritual torment of hell, of being shut out in some way we cannot picture, from His Father's approbation.

God Both Dead and Alive

Jesus Christ's paying for all of our sin through His death on the cross and His subsequent resurrection from the dead ranks as the most dramatic expression given to us of His control over all dimensional realms. Because He died, remained dead for "three days and three nights,"[22-23] and arose bodily from death to life, exactly as He predicted, proves that He has the power to *limit* any portion of His capacities and powers to any degree He chooses, whenever and wherever He chooses, and along whatever space-time dimensions (or super-dimensions) He chooses. The converse is also true. Jesus can *expand* any portion of His capacities and powers to any degree He chooses, whenever and wherever He chooses, and along whatever space-time dimensions (or super-dimensions) He chooses.

Some skeptics and atheists have argued that if Jesus were God, He could not have died; and if He died, He could not have been God. They recognize, of course, the contradiction in saying that Jesus is both really dead and really alive. Several famous nonbelievers have used this line of reasoning to conclude that the Christian faith is irrational and, therefore, unworthy of consideration.

The simultaneity of Jesus' death and immortality would only be a contradiction, however, if the time, place, and context of His death were identical to the time, place, and dimensional context of His being alive (see the discussion of contradictions and paradoxes in chapter 6 on pages 52-53). Even with respect to human death, we recognize the role of an extra-dimensional realm, though we may not use those words. Death, for us, refers to a change, a transition, a cessation of some kind, but it is not an annihilation (see chapter 16). While our physical death involves a definite and significant loss, that loss does not negate the possibility of a far greater extra-dimensional gain. Ultimately, we know our existence continues when our physical bodies can no longer sustain us.

The apostle John implies that the Holy Spirit communicates this fact to all;[24] though, of course, some in their rebellion against or practiced ignoring of God work very hard to deny it.[25] When we leave our familiar time and space abode and the physical bodies in which we were born, we enter some other realm or dimension(s), because our life extends beyond mere physical reality. While our physical body dies, our spirit continues to live. As the book of Ecclesiastes explains, eternity is somehow written on our hearts.[26]

Because of Christ's identity as God and His access to all the dimensions or super-dimensions God encompasses, He could experience suffering and death in all the human-occupied dimensions and then transition into any of His other dimensions or realms once the atonement price had been paid. Evidencing His divine nature, Jesus resisted the temptation to escape from the agonies of a torturous death and finalized the payment for all our sin.

Limited or Unlimited Payment

The debate over whether Christ's atonement was "limited" or "unlimited" arises from two misperceptions. One equates sin (singular, universal) with sins (plural, individual) and thus quantifies that something for which atonement is required. The other, connected with it, applies God's foreknowledge to that quantitative assumption. The Bible declares God knows even before we are conceived or the universe was created whether we will reject His offer of forgiveness for our sin(s).[27-28] According to one line of reasoning, the penalty for which payment is needed must be the penalty for the sin of those and only those whom He knows will accept His payment made on their behalf. The rationale here is that for Christ to pay for all the offenses for all humanity, and yet have only some humans receive the benefit of the payment, is tantamount to saying that Christ's payment is at least partially without effect. And for Christ to be in any way ineffective would mean He is less than omnipotent.

This argument correctly affirms Christ's omnipotence but stumbles into contradiction with many other passages of Scripture.

These three are typical:

Christ died for the ungodly.[29]

He [Jesus] suffered death, so that by the grace of God He might taste death for everyone.[30]

Jesus Christ, the Righteous One. He is the atoning sacrifice for our sins, and not only for ours but also for the sins of the whole world.[31]

The debate can be resolved, at least to some degree of satisfaction, by reconsidering the logic or validity of labeling "unaccepted pardon" as "ineffectual payment." To use a human example, if the court accepts my offer to pay the traffic fines for four of my friends, knowing that I can cover the maximum amount charged for their violations, my bank account and generosity are not limited nor adjudged insufficient should any of my friends refuse to accept my offer to pay their fines.

A complete resolution may be had if we accept that God had an important purpose in dying for everyone regardless of anyone's decision to receive or reject His offer of forgiveness. Christ may have died and paid the penalty for all so that no one could ever, at any future point, rightly conclude that God did not express His love toward that person. In a later chapter on hell's torment, we will look at the proposition that God continuously expresses His perfect love to all for the rest of eternity.

Resolving the deeper issue of humans' free will and how it can operate without contradicting God's sovereign will, and vice versa, would offer a much more deeply satisfactory answer. This resolution, which can be accomplished in extra-dimensional reality, will be addressed in a later chapter.

Adding Up the Price

The quantitative perspective on our atonement price and a four-dimensional view of what Christ endured on the cross have raised a target for secular skepticism and ridicule. The idea that one man's suffering for one afternoon on a Roman cross—a painful execution that many other men endured—could even approach equivalence to the eternal torment and suffering of the billions who have rejected or will reject His offer of redemption, seems absurd. Jesus' suffering on the cross lasted but six hours.[32] (The emotional and spiritual pain of knowing what He would endure began much earlier, of course, perhaps even before the angels and the universe were created. In this sense the agony of the Atonement began much before the Incarnation.) His suffering on the cross, though greater than what any other being has ever endured,[33] may at first glance seem finite and imaginable. How, then, could one imaginable experience of torment of apparently limited duration be equivalent to hell's unimaginable torment visited for an unimaginable duration on vast numbers of people?

Such reasoning overlooks the implications of Christ's simultaneous deity and humanity. His payment of our ransom price must be accounted for in a perspective that goes beyond our physical realm. The book of Hebrews offers this insight:

> He [Christ] went through the greater and more perfect tabernacle that is not man-made, that is to say, not a part of this creation.[34]

> Christ did not enter a man-made sanctuary that was only a copy of the true one; he entered heaven itself, now to appear for us in God's presence. Nor did he enter heaven to offer himself again and again, . . . Christ was sacrificed once to take away the sins of many people.[35]

A significant part of what transpired in Christ's payment of all that our death warrants took place in God's extra-dimensional realm. While Scripture is clear that all of our sins have been completely atoned for by Christ's one sacrifice,[36] it does not explain every detail of how the atonement price was accounted. What matters is that Jesus Christ has the capacity to make full payment. Our confidence rests in His adequacy.

Given even a limited understanding of Christ's extra-dimensional characteristics and powers, however, we can suggest some possible approaches to that accounting. Perhaps the easiest for us to comprehend would be reckoning Jesus' payment of our atonement price in two extra dimensions of time.

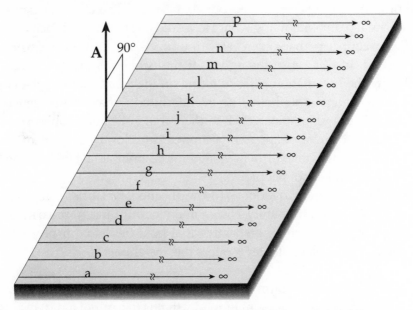

Figure 10.1: Paying the Atonement Price in Multiple Dimensions of Time
Line **A** represents the universe's time line. One of many ways Christ could atone for all the sins of humanity would be to pay the redemption price in two dimensions of time, completely independent of our time dimension. In this time plane, Christ could suffer for infinite time on billions of different time lines: **a**, **b**, **c**, etc. Thus, in a few moments on the cross in our time dimension, Jesus Christ could experience the payment for the sins of every human who has ever lived or will ever live.

The penalty for one person's sin—unimaginably painful torment and isolation from God and everything and everyone good and righteous forever—would require that individual's existence (after physical death on earth) on at least one infinitely long time line. If some twenty billion people incur sin's penalty, twenty billion infinite time lines would represent the cumulative total of sin's penalty. With a second time dimension, God could move along, that is, experience, these twenty billion lines. He would possess a plane of time that could encompass all of them (see figure 10.1). Thus, while Jesus suffered on the cross for six hours on our time line, He could have experienced the suffering of twenty billion infinite time-lines in two other dimensions of time.

There are other ways, of course, that Jesus could have experienced the fullness of hell's torment. Jesus could have used His superior capacities to experience intensified torment on a limited time scale. In other words, He could choose to suffer to an infinite degree for a finite time rather than to suffer a finite degree for infinite time. Either way, the sum total remains the same.

This minimal comprehension of what Christ endured to cover the consequences of all our sin can be numbingly overwhelming. But as we allow time for this numbness to wear off, we can experience anew, perhaps much more deeply than ever, gratitude and amazement at the magnitude of His love. And we may better understand the basis for this question in Hebrews: "How shall we escape if we ignore such a great salvation?"[37]

Does the Atonement Demote Christ?

Some Christians also express concern that the notion of Christ's infinitely intense or infinitely enduring payment for sin's penalty somehow diminishes Him in relation to God the Father and God the Holy Spirit. Their concern arises, perhaps, from our familiar, finite perspective. A finite supply of anything can be diminished by withdrawals or expenditures from that supply. However, even if the supply of some particular resource is limited, an expenditure of it in any amount, even the total, does nothing to demote or diminish the one who makes that expenditure. That individual's attributes and identity remain intact regardless of the generosity he or she might display.

God's relinquishing of time dimensions (or the equivalent) to atone for sin, if He actually did do so, would be incomparable to our giving up a dimension. For us humans to lose the capacity to operate in one of our four dimensions would be catastrophic. It would limit our functionality and either tremendously diminish the meaning of our personhood or eradicate it altogether. But, for God, the case is radically different. He can, as He has already demonstrated, create dimensions of time and space at will. While humanity is subject to whatever time and space dimensions He places us in, time and space are subject to Him. Although Christ did make an enormous expenditure of His resources in atoning for our sins, He could do so without depleting or diminishing His supply of power and resources and without altering His identity.

A brief review of the concept of infinity may help clarify this point. Infinity minus one still equals infinity. The psalmist declares that God owns "the cattle on a thousand hills."[38] Making a gift of all those cattle does not make God poor or poorer. His resources are infinite. Infinite wealth minus the cattle on a thousand hills still adds up to infinite wealth.

Does God's infinite wealth mean that any gift He gives us counts as nothing to Him? Can He really be considered "generous" if He experiences no depletion? To answer this question requires a contextual shift from the material realm to the nonmaterial. For example, does the giving of love or kindness or compassion deplete our supply of such things? It may deplete our time or energy or other resources, but not these intangibles. Because we still have more to give after we have given, does this eradicate the value of the giving? Hardly. In the same way, no matter how Christ paid for our sins, the gift amounts to more than we can imagine, and it takes nothing away from the equality He shares with God the Father and God the Holy Spirit.

Does the Atonement Permanently Mar Christ?

When the disciples were visited by the resurrected Christ, they were able to see and feel the wounds of His crucifixion.[39] Christ certainly had the power to eradicate these wounds, but He chose to let them remain. One reason may be that these marks were essential to convince the disciples of the reality of Jesus' bodily resurrection. The wounds identified Him as nothing else could have. And no doubt these marks helped remind the disciples of what the Creator willingly endured to atone for their sins and of the permanent effects of that atoning sacrifice. This kind of reminder may be of some benefit to future generations of disciples and even to the hosts of angels and demons.

Whether these marks of the cross will remain for us to see when we enter Christ's presence we do not know. The book of Revelation, which gives more description of the heavenly realm and of our future there than does any other portion of Scripture, gives no clear answer to this question. Yet we can speculate that when the magnificence of the new creation is revealed to us, and when we begin to fathom the loss and the horror that hell represents, we may well be sufficiently reminded of the magnitude of the price Christ paid for our atonement.

Beyond Our Imagining

The Incarnation is described in the second chapter of Philippians as Christ's becoming "nothing." Such a statement does not deny the wonder and worth of human beings, but it does express the magnitude of Christ's divestiture in accepting life as a human. The humility He demonstrated in coming to us and dying for us exemplifies the humility we need in coming to Him. His example of humility, rather than hinting at any weakness or inferiority, indicates just the opposite—the moral perfection of God alone.

The differences made by that one-dimensional gap between the screen people and us, as vast as they are, seem utterly trivial, "nothing," compared with the differences made by the seven- or more-dimensional gap between us and God. What is more, the Incarnation and the Atonement show us God's capacity to operate in any dimensional realm, any combination of space and time dimensions (or super dimensions) He chooses. He can also manifest different aspects of Himself in different dimensional realms. The reality in which He can live and move supersedes by far the limits of human imagination. And yet we know He wants us to try to imagine it, to anticipate our future in it, because He gave us sneak previews—in His Word, in His creation, in His Incarnation, and in His Atonement.

CHAPTER ELEVEN

DIMENSIONAL CAPACITIES OF CREATED BEINGS

So far our attention has been focused chiefly on the reality and ramifications of God's eleven or more space and time dimensions. Because God has the capacity to create and remove dimensions, He lives with no dimensional constraints whatever—except, of course, any self-imposed ones He deems appropriate to His purposes. The life forms He created have been designed for and placed within certain dimensional constraints, and these apparently differ from one life form to another. An exploration of the dimensional features of the different kinds of creatures may help us develop a deeper understanding and appreciation of how these various life forms, ourselves included, relate to each other and to God.

The first chapter of Genesis distinguishes four life forms, and other portions of Scripture identify three more: (1) plants; (2) animals; (3) animals with "soulish" characteristics; (4) humans, endowed with "soulish" characteristics and a spirit; (5) angels; (6) cherubim; and (7) archangels. The biblical terms and descriptions of these different forms appear below. While the descriptions used for Earth's life forms harmonize well with both the scientific order and scientific classifications, the categorization system was chosen to fit the purpose of the passage, to show how God prepared the way for His creation of humankind.

1. Plants (Hebrew words *eseb, zera, es, peri, deshe yereq*; Greek words *chortus, dendron, phuteia*): organisms rooted to some kind of soil and capable of using nutrients in the soil, water, and air to produce food. Plants exist in the space and time dimensions of the universe and are subject to its natural laws.

2. *Animals* (Hebrew words *sheres, daga*; Greek words *herpeton, icthus*): organisms devoid of any significant capacity to relate to human beings, except perhaps via the food chain. They have the capacity to move and reproduce, responding to instincts that foster their survival. They are dependent on plants (either directly through eating plants or indirectly through eating other animals) for their energy. These creatures exist in the space and time dimensions of the universe and are subject to its natural laws.

3. *Soulish animals* (Hebrew words *nephesh, hay, hayya, behema, remes, be'ir, basar, tannin, sippor, 'op, kanap*; Greek words *orneon, pteinon, ktenos, therion, zoon*): animals endowed with the capacity to relate to human beings and to one another at levels beyond mere instinct, with some degree of intelligence, emotion, and will. Soulish animals exist in the space and time dimensions of the universe and are subject to its natural laws.

4. *Humans* (Hebrew words *adam, enosh, ish*; Greek word *anthropos*): soulish creatures endowed with self-awareness and God-awareness, innate moral and ethical standards, and a proclivity for religious expression and exploration. Humans exist in the space and time dimensions of the universe and in a spiritual reality beyond those dimensions. They are subject to natural laws, social laws, and spiritual laws, and they bear responsibility for managing animal and plant life, as well as their own behavior.

5. *Angels* (Hebrew word *malak*; Greek word *angelos*): intelligent beings existing beyond the space and time dimensions of the universe, subject to spiritual laws but not necessarily to natural laws. One third, the fallen angels or demons, are in rebellion against God.[1] The remaining two-thirds bear responsibility for service to God and can, at His bidding, make contact with humans in the space and time dimensions of the universe.

6. *Cherubim* (Hebrew word *kerub*, singular, *-im*, plural; Greek word *cheroubim*): a special order of angelic beings with a unique role in directing and expressing worship toward God.

7. *Archangels* (Greek word *archangelos*): angels of exalted rank and power, sent by God to carry out special assignments.

The Plants

Plants are foundational to God's layering of life on the earth. Only plants can gain food from inorganic matter. While they are different from animals, they possess certain similarities, such as the capacity to respire and reproduce. Because plants are never referred to as "creatures" anywhere in the Bible, some Bible interpreters hold that plants are not alive and do not experience death.[2-4] Job contrasts a tree's vitality with a man's: "Its stump [may] die in the soil, yet at the scent of water it will bud. . . . But man dies and is laid low."[5] King David makes this comparison: "Like green plants they will soon die away."[6]

The Hebrew words for "death" used by Moses and Job denote the physical death of a living thing.[7]

While the Bible unmistakably refers to plants as living and dying organisms, it offers no support for the concept common to many eastern religions that plants share in a "cosmic consciousness." Scientific and biblical evidences establish that plants do respond to their environment for survival's sake, sending branches toward sunlight and roots toward water and nutrients. But nowhere in Scripture does God endow them with soul or spirit.

Jesus' curse on the fig tree may not be used to establish any conscious nature in plants.[8] As the Creator of the universe, Jesus has complete command over both the organic and inorganic world. His calming of the storm on the Sea of Galilee provides convincing evidence of such authoritative capacity.[9] Plants are strictly confined to the matter, energy, and the four space-time dimensions of the universe. They cannot form relationships with animals or humans. They manifest none of the attributes identified with the soul or the spirit.

The Animals

Animal life manifests enormous diversity of size, form, mobility, food-getting mechanisms, reproductive processes, respiration, adaptability, longevity, etc. Bible authors categorize them in the general terms appropriate to the text's focus on relationships, responsibilities, and redemption, and not always in the precise terms of scientific methodology. Sometimes wild animals are distinguished from those man easily makes pets of or domesticates. Sometimes animals that do not communicate or interact with humans in any relational way are distinguished from those that do. Mollusks, fish, amphibians, and insects, for example, tend to be grouped (among others) in the non-relational category, if and when the biblical context indicates that such a distinction is being made.

Just as with plants, the Bible refers to these non-relational animals as experiencing life and death. The Lord instructed Moses to tell Pharaoh, "The fish in the Nile will die."[10] Later, Moses records the death of fish[11] and, later still, the death of frogs.[12] Solomon describes the laudable behavior and other characteristics of ants[13] and refers to the death of flies.[14]

Animals differ from the plants in that they possess the capacity to obtain and digest food rather than to manufacture it. Since they are not typically rooted to the soil or to other vegetation as plants are, most can freely roam the environs of their land or ocean habitat (and in some cases, both). However, they share with the plants the following characteristics: (1) confinement to the matter, energy, and four space-time dimensions of the universe; and (2) incapacity (of most species) to display emotion or to respond to the emotions of other creatures.

The Soulish Animals

The Bible singles out certain animal species or kinds from others. The distinction first becomes apparent in the Genesis creation accounts. In referring to some creatures, ones we might call "higher animals," the author uses the Hebrew noun *nephesh*. This word singles out "soulish" creatures from other animals by their capacity to form what may be described as emotional attachments to other animals and to human beings.[15] God created certain species with capacities for interaction at levels involving intelligence, choice, and emotions. Their special characteristics inspire humans to tame, domesticate, train, and make enjoyable pets of various types of birds and mammals. Humans make pets of other creatures, too, such as frogs, turtles, snakes, and iguanas, for example, but the relationship possibilities with such pets are essentially one way.

In recording the account of God's creation of these soulish animals, Moses uses the Hebrew verbs *asa* and *bara*. According to Hebrew lexicons, *asa* means "manufacture" or "fabricate," and its sense implies God's action in fashioning the creature.[16] *Bara* carries the strong sense of "create," of bringing into existence something new, something that has not previously existed.[17] The biblical text suggests that God personally designed the bodies of these advanced creatures and placed within them some capacity no other earthly creature had possessed previously—a capacity that the Old Testament writers using Hebrew could call a "soul." But this Hebrew "soul" must not be confused with the New Testament Greek concept of "soul," which in many biblical contexts encompasses what the Hebrew would identify as "spirit."[18]

Scripture suggests that the soulishness of birds and mammals gives them the capacity to detect the presence of extra-dimensional beings if and when those beings influence the physical or emotional realm they enter. Balaam's ass, for example, was aware of an angelic visitor even when Balaam was not.[19] Individuals who have observed occult practices, which often involve encounters with demons (fallen angels), reported that a bird or a mammal may react visibly or audibly to the demonic visitation, while other animals, such as reptiles, make no response. The most likely explanation for soulish animals' sensitivity to the presence of demons arises from their sensitivity to people's physical cues, to changes of movement, expression, or even odor, however subtle. Both angels and demons are described in Scripture as capable of impacting our dimensional realm, becoming visible, audible, or tangible some other way. Soulish animals' ability to detect these spiritual beings says more, perhaps, about the abilities of angels and demons to communicate with soulish creatures than about soulish creatures' detection capacity.

Whatever the case, soulish creatures cannot be said to possess spiritual capacities. None of these animal species has ever been observed to engage in worship or to practice any form of religion. Grieving the loss of a life partner, burying the dead, or decorating a nest with trinkets expresses emotional capacity, not a spiritual capacity, for these creatures. Their behavior gives no indication of any awareness of a conscience or of a moral code. Neither do they display any concern over the existence of a Creator or of life beyond physical death. By all indications, when soulish animals die, they return to the dust. They do not possess ongoing spiritual or extra-dimensional life. This statement does not mean necessarily that none of these wonderful animal species will exist in the new creation. The Bible is silent on this issue. But it does suggest that if such creatures are present, they will not be the ones that lived with us here on Earth. Nevertheless, we have solid evidence that God cares for these creatures. The psalmist says,

> These all look to you
>> to give them their food at the proper time.
> When you give it to them,
>> they gather it up;
> when you open your hand,
>> they are satisfied with good things.[20]

Jesus indirectly admonishes people to care for their animals on the Sabbath, as on any other day,[21] and He addresses the disciples' fears about evil befalling them with reference to God's awareness of a tiny bird: "Are not two sparrows sold for a penny? Yet not one of them will fall to the ground apart from the will of your Father."[22]

The Spirit Beings
According to Genesis, God created only one species of life on Earth with a capacity called "spirit." Just as with the soulish animals, the wording of the passage indicates the introduction of some new and unique life form. For God's final work of creation, the narrator chooses the Hebrew noun, *adam*, and again he uses the Hebrew verbs *asa* and *bara* to depict the creative act. "Adam" refers exclusively to the earthly creature (both male and female) God endowed with a special capacity to communicate with and relate to Him.[23] The use of *asa* and *bara* again imply that God personally designed the physical and soulish characteristics of the first human and that He did something entirely new in endowing that human with a "spirit."

The human spirit manifests itself, at least in part, by humans' unique consciousness. While no reputable scholar disputes that human beings are uniquely conscious beings, many scholars hesitate or refuse to give God credit for that conscious nature. Some of this generation's most brilliant researchers have tried valiantly to find within matter, energy, and the natural biochemical processes of our space and time dimensions a hypothesis for the origin and operation of human consciousness, but none of their efforts has come close to succeeding.[24-26] In fact, their findings only help build the case for a supernatural origin.

Spirit beings, whatever their level of intelligence, manifest a capacity that not even the most highly intelligent soulish animals possess, the ability to discern dimensions beyond the ones we physically experience. We may even interact and dialogue, knowingly or not, with spiritual beings from beyond our physically experienced dimensions. According to the Bible, human beings may sometimes be allowed to see, hear, interact and dialogue with angels, mistaking them for humans. In the book of Hebrews we are exhorted, "Do not forget to entertain strangers, for by so doing some people have entertained angels without knowing it."[27] Sometimes people know, or come to recognize, angels as messengers from the spiritual, or extra-dimensional realm, as we see in accounts of Abraham's, Lot's, and Daniel's interactions with angels.[28]

Because we are spiritual beings, we humans can pray. Through prayer we can cross the space-time manifold of the cosmos and converse with God in His extra-dimensional realm. Because prayer is extra-dimensional in its reach, it must be considered the most powerful capacity God has made available to us in our current dimensional context. Prayer is so powerful, it comes with special cautions and restrictions on its use.[29]

Again, because we are spirit beings, we humans, alone among all earthly creatures, possess the capacity to experience life beyond physical death, life that survives outside the physical body we now occupy. God says we will witness His eventual creation of a new universe to replace this one. The new one will function with different physical laws and occupy different space-time dimensions (see chapter 17). Because we humans are spirit beings, we can make this transition to life beyond our earthly body and earthly dimensions, either life without end in the new creation (see chapter 17) or death without end in the lake of fire (see chapter 16).

All human beings—men, women, and children, in all geographical and historical contexts—possess innate knowledge not instilled by human instruction but by our Creator. Whether our family and culture affirm these beliefs or deny them, humans gradually become aware of these things:

+ Truth exists and does not change.[30]
+ Life continues forever after death.[31]
+ God deserves our worship, for His standard and His law are perfection.[32]
+ We cannot live up to God's perfect standard.[33]
+ God knows our heart, the core of our being, and will judge (evaluate) us after our earthly life is over.[34]

Those of us who invite God's Spirit to live in the core of our being and to express Christ through us—body, soul, and spirit—become linked forever with God. We experience a change as dramatic as birth, and it is called a spiritual birth. God's character and capacities become available to us as never before, despite the necessary limits of our physical context. From the time this spiritual birth takes place, we begin a never-ending process of growth in love, joy, peace, patience, kindness, goodness, faithfulness, gentleness, and self-control, among other Christlike qualities.[35]

We still need to nourish and maintain our body and soul. Our human bodies keep us subject to the laws of thermodynamics and gravity, for example. We need food, rest, exercise, work, relationships, and recreation. To take care of ourselves is tantamount to caring for "the temple of the living God."[36] Such a comment should inspire us to do a good job. Personal neglect does not please Him. Meanwhile, God provides the nourishment that sustains our spirit. We have constant access to it, and it is just as important to our spiritual health as breathing oxygen or drinking water is to our physical sustenance. Elihu reminds us in the book of Job, "If it were his intention and he withdrew his Spirit and breath, all mankind would perish together and man would return to the dust."[37]

God wants to provide so much more than physical and spiritual vitality. For those who commit their lives to Him and invite His

Spirit to live within, He supplies both the desire and the power to fulfill His purposes here on Earth,[38] an assignment that yields for each of us what He describes as "life to the full."[39] Jesus spoke to His disciples about this life:

> "I tell you the truth, if you have faith as small as a mustard seed, you can say to this mountain, 'Move from here to there' and it will move. Nothing will be impossible for you."[40]

> "I tell you the truth, if you have faith and do not doubt, not only can you do what was done to the fig tree, but also you can say to this mountain, 'Go, throw yourself into the sea,' and it will be done. If you believe, you will receive whatever you ask for in prayer."[41]

> "I tell you the truth, anyone who has faith in me will do what I have been doing. He will do even greater things than these, because I am going to the Father. And I will do whatever you ask in my name, so that the Son may bring glory to the Father. You may ask me for anything in my name, and I will do it. If you love me, you will obey what I command."[42]

Learning to use our extra-dimensional capacities takes time, for it takes growth in faith, with accompanying wisdom and purity. In asking for "anything," that "anything" must be identified by a heart attuned to God's purposes and plans.[43] How often are we inclined to ask for the removal of trouble from our path? And yet He told us clearly that trouble is a constant companion, a tool for character growth, during our earthly life:

> "In this world you will have trouble. But take heart! I have overcome the world."[44]

Knowing what to ask in the face of trouble comes through knowing Him better and better. Building any relationship takes effort and attention, and the same is true of our relationship with

God. The attention is always fully available on His part; our part is up to us. The apostle Paul tells us that our developing relationship with the Lord can bring such daily renewal and radiance that it overshadows the troubles and even the aging process in our lives.

> And we, who with unveiled faces all reflect the Lord's glory, are being transformed into his likeness with ever-increasing glory, which comes from the Lord, who is the Spirit.[45]

> Therefore we do not lose heart. Though outwardly we are wasting away, yet inwardly we are being renewed day by day. For our light and momentary troubles are achieving for us an eternal glory that far outweighs them all. So we fix our eyes not on what is seen, but on what is unseen. For what is seen is temporary, but what is unseen is eternal.[46]

Angels

The angels we see in paintings and sculptures typically have feminine or childlike features, golden halos, and wings ranging from tiny to grandiose. Many artistic portrayals more closely resemble the traditional image of Cupid than they do the biblical description of angels. The Bible tells us they are mighty[47] and holy.[48] It says they are mightier than we humans are.[49] They are so swift as to defy the laws of physics.[50] They are subject neither to decay nor to death. They can be visible or invisible to humans.[51] In most biblically recorded cases of their appearance on Earth, the people who saw and heard them responded with terror. The following account by Daniel illustrates an angel's impact:

> As I was standing on the bank of the great river, the Tigris, I looked up and there before me was a man dressed in linen, with a belt of the finest gold around his waist. His body was like chrysolite, his face like lightning, his eyes like flaming torches, his arms and legs like the gleam of burnished bronze, and his voice like the sound of a multitude.
>
> I, Daniel, was the only one who saw the vision; the men with me did not see it, but such terror overwhelmed them

that they fled and hid themselves. So I was left alone, gazing at this great vision; I had no strength left, my face turned deathly pale and I was helpless.[52]

Daniel then explains that when the angel started speaking, he (Daniel) passed out, and the angel had to help him to his feet. The angel's purpose in coming to Daniel was to give him a message about the future, to let him know what is written in "the Book of Truth," as the angel called it. The angel also reported his intense conflict with a fallen angel, specifically with the demon who held some measure of authority over Persia. This demon had the power to detain the angel for twenty-one days.

From these biblical accounts and others, we learn that angels' capacities reflect their existence in at least some of God's dimensions outside the four of the universe. Compared to God, however, angels are limited. The Bible indicates that God alone is omnipotent, omniscient, and omnipresent. Angels are not.[53] Though they have access to more dimensions than we humans do, they occupy a limited dimensionality, as we do. Though they are able to exercise extraordinary power,[54] they are created beings, as we are, incapable of creating any other beings.[55] Unlike humans, they do not marry or procreate,[56] though some Bible scholars interpret a few passages of Scripture as suggesting that fallen angels in one way or another, and for a limited time, demonstrated the capacity to produce "mutant" offspring through sexual relations with human women.[57]

Cherubim, Seraphim, and Archangels

God apparently endowed certain angelic beings with power and authority above others. Though many "ranks" of angels may exist,[58] the Bible mentions but three.

The highest order appears to be the *cherubim.* Satan, identified as the most powerful and exalted of all the angels—before his rebellion—was a cherub.[59] No beings in all Scripture, other than God Himself, give observers a more difficult descriptive task. Depictions by the prophet Ezekiel[60] and the apostle John[61] represent arduous attempts to portray extra-dimensional features that far surpass what we humans can comprehend or imagine and far surpass the capacities and attributes shared by the lower ranks of angels. The cherubim alone are entrusted with certain tasks in protecting God's glory and holiness and in proclaiming His grace. What all these tasks entail we cannot yet begin to imagine.

Seraphim is a Hebrew term for "burning ones."[62] This title probably refers neither to fire as we know it nor to the consuming judgment. Rather, it expresses the passionate devotion of a particular order of angelic beings to praise and proclaim to all creation God's holiness and majesty. Though these angels, too, are awesome to behold, they pose at least a little less difficulty for humans to describe than do the cherubim.[63]

It is possible that God created more than one *archangel*.[64] However, only one, Michael, is mentioned by name in the Bible.[65] His specific role is perhaps most comparable to that of a military leader. He is the commander who leads the angelic host against Satan's demonic forces. Michael's ultimate victory over Satan[66] suggests that his powers and abilities may at least approximate Satan's.

Roles Now and Later

When we read of the awesome powers and attributes angels possess, we may wonder why God would describe us as "a little lower than the heavenly beings" or "angels."[67] Though the dimensionality and capacities of the angels supersede ours by what seems a vast margin, we have the opportunity and capacity to comprehend certain spiritual realities that mystify angels.[68] In the life that continues past our physical death, we humans who choose to worship Christ will be assigned as "judges" (leaders) and teachers of the angels.[69]

For now, one of the roles God has assigned to angels is to help provide for our protection. The more we need, due to age, other dependency factors, and spiritual circumstances, the more we get.[70] God also deploys angels to perform supernatural acts of service on behalf of those individuals who devote their lives fully to spreading the gospel (the good news of what Jesus has offered to humanity) and equipping others to do the same.[71]

CHAPTER TWELVE

GOD'S OMNIPOTENCE VERSUS HIS DISPLAYED POWER

Anyone who has ever taken a philosophy class has probably heard this question: Can God create a rock so massive that He cannot lift it? If we answer that He can create such a rock, we admit God's inability to lift or move the rock and thus imply He is less than all-powerful. If we say He cannot create such a rock, then we declare Him limited in His creative abilities. If we identify the impasse as a contradiction we must live with, a knot that cannot be untangled, we imply that God may not be consistent logically and is not totally truthful. With this little puzzle, many a non-theist has excused his or her denial or ignoring of God's existence, and many a student has grown less confident about his or her Christian faith.

This "proof" against God takes various forms. One that virtually all believers have faced at one time or another is the "proof" that God must not care or must not be adequately powerful or He would put a stop to evil and suffering. A later chapter will address this particular argument, but we can lay a foundation for that discussion by considering the core fallacy in such challenges to God's omnipotence.

Cannot Versus Will Not

The problem arises in part from a semantic issue, a misuse of the little word *can*, and in part from a nearsighted perspective. It seems far more appropriate to ask questions about what God *will* do than about what He *can* do, especially given the "can-do" He demonstrated so amply in the creation.

Some things God will not do. In one sense, He cannot do these things, but the reason has nothing to do with a power limitation. Rather, He cannot do certain things because He is powerful enough and righteous enough to choose not to do them ever. God cannot lie or distort the truth.[1] He cannot do evil.[2] He cannot accept evil.[3] Nor can He ever overlook evil.[4]

Why can He not do these things? He cannot because He is perfectly consistent. His character is immutable; it simply does not change.[5] His perfection, holiness, love, truthfulness, goodness, and faithfulness (among many other attributes) remain unchanged and unchangeable. They do not begin and end because He does not begin and end. His unchanging character reveals His power, a power that we do not possess, to maintain complete character consistency. He is not subject to the immaturity, ignorance, lack of love, shortsightedness, or genetic and chemical factors that influence our judgments, decisions, and actions and so often render them inconsistent. We could say He has the power to maintain Himself perfect with perfect self-control.

God's Freedom to Refrain

Time and again, we humans are tempted by our own impatience to question God's inaction. We cannot fathom why He does not intervene in the affairs of humans, preventing or overruling their wrong choices with a display of His extra-dimensional powers. The irony of our question might be humorous if it were not so terribly arrogant. We must ask ourselves how sensible it is for us humans to stand in judgment over what God will or will not do and when He will or will not do it given the immeasurable differences between His moral character and ours, His power and ours, His dimensional perspective and ours, His love and ours.

The Benefit of Moral Perfection

How often have we heard skeptics say, "If God is good, why did He . . . ?" or "why didn't He . . . ?" In asking this question, the inquirer has either knowingly or unwittingly exalted his or her judgment of what is good, what is warranted, over God's knowledge of such things. The inquirer implies that God's goodness cannot be believed or trusted.

Jesus set the record straight on this matter when He was approached by a self-righteous religious leader who flatteringly addressed Him as "good teacher."[6] With penetrating insight into the man's puffed up self-evaluation, Jesus replied, "Why do you call me good?"[7] Then He added, "No one is good — except God alone."[7] Jesus' statement affirms a truth revealed throughout Scripture, as well as throughout nature: God is the one and only source and essence of goodness. What He created He declared "good," and He encourages us to do "good" to both our friends and enemies; but goodness emanates from and is ultimately defined by Him alone.

From a mathematical and dimensional perspective, the Creator's goodness may be described as infinite. Though we humans have the capacity as spirit beings to recognize and express to some degree His goodness, we have no capacity for goodness apart from Him. If God did not exist, or if God were not good, we would not even know such a quality were possible.

The Benefit of Power

How often have we heard skeptics say, "If God is good, then He must be weak, otherwise He would. . . ." Again, some fundamental fallacious assumptions lie behind the challenge.

One of the fallacies is the expressed certainty that we can discern the absolute best course of action in a particular situation. All we can really know of absolutes is that they must exist, for God exists. While God has absolute knowledge of everything, we humans possess absolute knowledge of nothing because of our finite limits (see chapter 4).

A second fallacy lies in our mistaking the exercise of power as the measure of available power. A limited expression of power or a restraint of action cannot be used to indicate what power is possible and available. It cannot be used to infer weakness or lack of power. If we see a well-muscled man carrying a twenty-pound backpack along the trail, we would not reasonably conclude that twenty pounds is the maximum load he has the strength to carry. We would demonstrate better logic in concluding that for today's outing, he needs only twenty pounds' worth of supplies. And what if he were to put down his pack for a while as he stops to take pictures or to do a little fishing? Could we reasonably assume that he has lost his strength to carry the pack, that it has suddenly become too heavy for him? A better guess says he does not have reason to carry it right now, but he can and will pick it up again when the time is right.

If God chooses to refrain from exercising a power that He showed He possesses in creating the space and time dimensions, the matter and energy, and the physical laws of the universe, we have no basis for assuming He no longer possesses that immeasurable power or is no longer willing to exercise it. We can only infer that His exercise of that power is subject to His choice. He can and will use it however, wherever, and whenever His goodness and other character attributes direct.

The Benefit of Perspective

"Timing is everything" may exaggerate the case, but the point of this familiar expression merits attention. Who of us has not learned the hard way that right actions at the wrong time thwart our efforts and our purposes? If a man decides to help his wife by making dinner for her, he has done a good thing—assuming he knows how to cook and what she likes. But if he does this right and good thing on an evening when she has plans to eat out, his efforts will probably fail to accomplish the purpose for which they were intended. Perhaps he did not ask, or perhaps she did not tell him when he did ask, but in either case, he lacks the ability to read her mind. He needs tangible clues.

Because God possesses the equivalent of at least one more time dimension than we human beings do, and because His space or other dimensions give Him a complete view of us, inside and out, we can be confident of His timing in exercising His powers and capacities. He not only has the goodness and the power, but also the knowledge and perspective, to time His actions perfectly. As the apostle Peter wrote, "The Lord is not slow in keeping His promise, as some understand slowness."[8] His timing will be based not only on what He knows about us individually in any given moment but also on what He knows about the entire human race and all the angelic hosts for all time(s) in our current dimensions and beyond.

A swift and loving resolution to the problem of evil and suffering, thus, must certainly be within God's grasp and must be part of His plan. So far, however, we have said nothing about God's specific strategies and means for eradicating evil and suffering. That we will address in chapter 15.

The Ultimate Goal

Scripture tells us that "God is love,"[9] and the creation testifies to that truth. As with goodness, God Himself gives meaning to the word. He is love's source and essence. Humanity's hunger for love, a higher love than we can know in any human relationship—as wonderful as that human love can be—reflects a universal hunger for God. The more love we experience in this life, the keener our anticipation for the love that awaits us in His domain, in His tangible presence.

Whatever love is, we know we want more of it to give and to receive. But our dimensional boundaries hem us in. Loving takes time, because loving takes knowing; and knowing, for us, takes time. Our three-dimensional bodies for now contain, and in some ways conceal, a more-dimensional or extra-dimensional being, a spiritual being. When we transition to the more-dimensional or extra-dimensional realm, we will gain new capacities for knowing and thus new capacities for loving.

But whatever love is, both here in these dimensions and there in our future home with God, we know it involves choice. Love cannot be coerced and still be love. It cannot be programmed and still be love. If it is not given freely by choice, it is something else, such as duty, and we yearn to give and receive so much more than obligatory care.

Since love involves choice, it also involves risks. In the chapter ahead, we will consider the paradox of an omniscient, omnipotent God who risks giving humanity, and the angels, too, real freedom of choice so that real love is possible. And yet He never relinquishes or compromises His sovereign control. This statement of the two truths side by side strikes our minds as a contradiction, or perhaps as an inscrutable mystery, because it is a mysterious contradiction—in four space-time dimensions. But remember, we have discovered that there are more than just those four.

Knowing God's reality encompasses more than four space-time dimensions, we can rejoice, too, that God has something better than Eden in store for us. As beautiful and pleasant as Eden must have been for Adam and Eve before they turned from God's way to their own, God's goal for humanity far surpasses an earthly paradise. He awaits the moment when He will escort us, who choose to enter, into the new creation. Building and maintaining the new creation involves more of God's extra-dimensional capacities than did Eden. It will involve much more than just our dimensions, too. The new creation is majestic, rewarding, and enduring beyond anything we can think or imagine. When we read the Bible writers' attempts to describe it, we know that the wonders of the place can never be exaggerated.

We will consider some of the specifics of the new creation in chapter 17. However, an appropriate appreciation of those specifics is only possible given a satisfactory resolution of pertinent aspects of the paradoxes of our free-will choices versus God's plans and control; whether believers can be eternally secure in their commitment to God; evil and suffering versus God's love and power; and God's love versus eternal torment in hell. Before considering the glory, majesty, and reward of the new creation, we will devote a chapter to each of these issues.

CHAPTER THIRTEEN

EXTRA-DIMENSIONALITY
AND THE BATTLE OF WILLS

We Christians would be hard pressed to identify a doctrine that has caused more difficulty and division in the church through the centuries than the one declaring whose will—human beings' or God's—holds sway in our lives. Many Scripture verses either declare directly or imply that we humans have the freedom to make choices for our lives, including the choice of whether to worship and serve God, and we bear responsibility for our choices. Many other verses declare or imply that God has control over all things that occur in this dimensional realm and beyond, and that He has predetermined, even before the universe was created, every aspect of human existence (all of our actions, words, and thoughts) to fit His overarching plan for eternity. In some cases, both sides of this seemingly contradictory message appear together in a single passage. A list of these verses appears in table 13.1 (page 136).

One of the most widely quoted passages emphasizing the power of human choice occurs in Joshua's final speech. On entering and occupying the promised land, Joshua exhorts the Israelite people to make the most important of all choices:

Now fear the LORD and serve him with all faithfulness.
Throw away the gods your forefathers worshiped beyond
the River and in Egypt, and serve the LORD. But if serving
the LORD seems undesirable to you, then choose for your-
selves this day whom you will serve, whether the gods
your forefathers served beyond the River, or the gods of the

Amorites, in whose land you are living. But as for me and my household, we will serve the LORD.[1]

When the people declare their choice to serve God, Joshua (strangely) warns them, "You are not able to serve the LORD."[2] Then a few moments later he tells them they will be held accountable for their choice to serve Him.[3] How can this be?

Table 13.1: Bible Verses Teaching Human Free-Will (F) and God's Predestination (P)

Gen. 13:11 (F)	Eccl. 3:10-17 (P&F)	John 7:17 (F)
Ex. 9:16 (P)	Eccl. 9:1 (P)	John 8:31-47 (P&F)
Ex. 33:19 (P)	Is. 1:29 (F)	John 10:26-29 (P&F)
Ex. 34:24 (P)	Is. 7:15-16 (F)	John 15:5 (P)
Deut. 10:15 (P)	Is. 40:20 (F)	John 15:16 (P)
Deut. 30:19 (F)	Is. 40:23 (P)	John 17:6 (P&F)
Josh. 11:20 (P)	Is. 41:24 (P)	Acts 2:21 (F)
Josh. 24:14-27 (F)	Is. 46:10 (P)	Acts 4:28 (P)
Judg. 5:8 (F)	Is. 55:3 (F)	Acts 13:48 (P&F)
Judg. 21:25 (F)	Is. 55:6-11 (P&F)	Acts 17:24-28 (P&F)
1 Kings 12:15 (P)	Is. 56:4 (F)	Rom. 4:11 (P)
2 Chr. 6:3-6 (P)	Is. 61:10–62:2 (P)	Rom. 8:19-33 (P)
Job 1:21-22 (P&F)	Jer. 1:4-10 (P)	Rom. 9:10-26 (P)
Job 7:15 (F)	Jer. 8:4-12 (F)	Rom. 10:12-18 (P&F)
Job 9:1-35 (P&F)	Jer. 17:5-10 (P&F)	Rom. 11:7-8 (P)
Job 23:10-16 (P&F)	Ezek. 18:1-32 (F)	Rom. 11:25–12:2 (P&F)
Job 34:4 (F)	Dan. 4:4-37 (P)	1 Cor. 1:2 (P)
Job 36:21 (F)	Hos. 4:4-9 (F)	1 Cor. 1:26-29 (P)
Job 38:36 (P&F)	Hos. 5:3-7 (P&F)	1 Cor. 4:7 (P)
Psalm 14:1-3 (F)	Hos. 11:4 (P)	1 Cor. 6:19-20 (P&F)
Psalm 25:12 (P&F)	Joel 2:32 (P&F)	2 Cor. 3:4-6 (P)
Psalm 31:15 (P)	Matt. 10:22 (P&F)	2 Cor. 13:9 (P)
Psalm 32:5-11 (P&F)	Matt. 10:28-30 (P)	Gal. 1:1 (P)
Psalm 33:8-22 (P&F)	Matt. 11:25 (P)	Eph. 1:4-5 (P)
Psalm 58:3 (P)	Matt. 21:21-22 (F)	Eph. 1:11 (P)
Psalm 110:1-7 (P)	Matt. 24:24-25 (P)	Eph. 2:10 (P)
Psalm 115:3 (P)	Matt. 24:36 (P)	Phil. 2:12-13 (P&F)
Psalm 119:30 (F)	Mark 13:20-22 (P)	2 Thess. 2:7-12 (P&F)
Psalm 119:173 (F)	Luke 8:10 (P)	2 Thess. 2:13-15 (P&F)
Prov. 1:29-30 (F)	Luke 10:42 (F)	2 Thess. 3:3 (P)
Prov. 8:10-19 (F)	Luke 12:4-5 (P)	1 Tim. 6:19 (F)
Prov. 16:4 (P)	Luke 18:27 (P)	2 Tim. 1:9 (P)
Prov. 16:9 (P&F)	Luke 22:21-22 (P&F)	2 Tim. 1:12 (P&F)
Prov. 21:1 (P)	Luke 22:31-34 (P)	2 Tim. 2:19-26 (P&F)
Prov. 21:3 (F)	John 6:44-65 (P&F)	Titus 1:1-3 (P)

Titus 2:11-14 (P)	Heb. 13:21 (P)	1 John 2:5-6 (F)
Heb. 3:4 (P)	James 1:13-25 (P&F)	1 John 3:9 (P)
Heb. 3:12-14 (F)	James 4:7 (F)	1 John 4:7-19 (P&F)
Heb. 4:11 (F)	James 4:13-17 (P)	1 John 5:18-20 (P)
Heb. 6:4-12 (F)	1 Pet. 1:4-5 (P)	Jude 1-4 (P&F)
Heb. 6:17-19 (P&F)	1 Pet. 1:15-16 (P&F)	Rev. 13:8-10 (P)
Heb. 10:14 (P)	1 Pet. 2:21 (F)	Rev. 20:11-15 (F)
Heb. 10:35 (P&F)	1 Pet. 5:5-10 (P&F)	Rev. 22:11-17 (F)
Heb. 11:25 (F)	2 Pet. 1:10 (P&F)	

Even before this moment, the mystery had been introduced. In a dialogue with Moses, God says that His Presence will go with the Hebrews in their journey, as Moses requests. Why? Perhaps He has always planned to go, but the reason He gives centers on Moses. He is going in answer to Moses' request because He knows Moses and is pleased with him. Then the focus turns to the Lord's sovereign decision and plan. The Lord says, "I will have mercy on whom I will have mercy, and I will have compassion on whom I will have compassion."[4] Human decision and action seem irrelevant in this declaration. But how can they be, if we humans bear accountability for our choices?

Other puzzling statements appear in the New Testament. One of the briefest comes from Luke in his account of the church's earliest days. When Gentiles respond to the message of salvation preached by Paul and Barnabas, he writes, "All who were appointed for eternal life believed."[5] Did these people believe because they were chosen to do so, or were they appointed to eternal life because God knew ahead of time that they would choose to believe?

Most believers and churches will answer that question with an emphasis on either the human decision-maker or the divine one. We know that actual contradictions cannot exist since God and His Word speak truth and only truth. So, we respond to these apparently incompatible statements by selecting to put on a pair of interpretive glasses that help us "adjust" the troubling texts one way or another as we encounter them.

Especially since the great debates between John Calvin's and Jacobus Arminius's adherents, these glasses have been available in two colors. One color highlights humanity's freedom of choice; the other, God's sovereign choice. And that is how Christians have typically dealt with the issue ever since. Arguments, even leading to bloodshed, ensued. In these slightly more civilized times, we simply agree to disagree and divide ourselves among the free-will congregations and the "election," or pre-determinist, congregations. Rarely are the twain willing to meet for dialogue or for worship side by side.

As a law of nature and of the Spirit, we recognize that distorting a message will yield further distortion down the line. Any distortion of God's truth about personal choice and responsibility will influence a person's and a church's walk of faith, the approach to spiritual growth and to making disciples in families, workplaces, neighborhoods, and the nations.

Individuals and churches highlighting the free-will side of the issue tend to emphasize what they may refer to as "holy living," or "separation from evil." Those on the other side of the issue may term such a perspective "legalism," or "rules of righteousness." The individuals and churches highlighting God's sovereign choice tend to emphasize what they might call "freedom in Christ" or "grace living." Those on the other side of the issue might term this approach "license."

In the past ten years or so, a group of believers from widely diverse church backgrounds has worked with me to compile two lists. These lists recount some attitudes and perspectives typifying one emphasis or the other. One opinion all these people shared: They had been hampered in their spiritual growth by the subtle one-sidedness. (See tables 13.2 and 13.3, pages 138 and 139. Add to them as you see fit, for they are personal perspectives.)

Table 13.2: Symptoms of Overemphasis on Free Will
Typically, when a person or fellowship stresses too much humans' will and not enough God's will in the spiritual birth and growth processes, the results include (a) working to please God or justify ourselves before Him by being good and doing good; and (b) viewing sin as so dangerously and powerfully enticing as to need policing by rigid, external, manmade restraints. Specific ways these distortions manifest themselves include the following, among others:

1. Life seems increasingly exhausting and draining rather than joyous and fulfilling.
2. Fear nags—fear that one has not done enough good things or fear that one has done too many bad things, or both.

3. Doubt nags—especially doubt about whether one is really saved, or will stay saved.
4. Supernatural gifts of the Spirit seem more important than the fruit of the Spirit because they appear to attest more dramatically to the Spirit's indwelling presence and to God's approval.
5. Conformity to certain behavior patterns, non-essential scriptural interpretations, or rules of conduct and expression become important validations of salvation.
6. Teaching focuses more on God's standards and justice than on His mercy. Assurance of salvation seems a dangerous door to temptation.
7. The distinction between justification and sanctification appears blurred.
8. Emotional expression, whether the glum extreme or the happy extreme, is taken as a sign of spirituality.
9. Prayers implore instant deliverance from immorality, addictions, and other long-term problems and ailments.
10. Shame lingers and seeks some form of anesthetic.
11. Weaknesses and struggles must be hidden from self and others or attributed to Satan's attacks.
12. The letter of the law receives more attention than the spirit of the law.
13. "Perfect" obedience rather than daily spiritual growth becomes life's goal.
14. Parents, teachers, and church leaders often seek control and justify it.
15. Fear of wrong choices leads to preference for "signs," strongly enforced prohibitions, and relinquishing choice to others, especially to authority figures.

Table 13.3: Symptoms of Overemphasis on Predestination
Typically, when a person or fellowship stresses too much God's will and not enough humans' will in the spiritual birth and growth processes, the results include (a) mistaking God's "grace" for freedom to do as one pleases; (b) minimizing temptation's power and sin's consequences.

1. Life in Christ seems much the same as any "good" person's life, but with the benefit of an eternal life insurance policy.
2. The initial step or indication of salvation, such as water baptism, confirmation, applying for church membership, or "coming forward," receives more attention than the ongoing process of growth.
3. Teaching emphasizes the mercy and forgiveness of God over the justice of God and losses resulting from sin.
4. Sermons focus more on comfort and assurance than on conviction, confession, and change. Hell is rarely if ever mentioned.
5. The role of the Holy Spirit in empowering believers for godly living receives little attention.
6. Distinctions between sanctification and glorification seem blurred.
7. God's plans become more His than ours to fulfill. The need for evangelists, missionaries, and counselors and for good teaching in apologetics and theology is downplayed.

8. Parents and church leaders take a fatalistic approach toward the spiritual life of family and church members and outsiders.
9. Immorality, addictions, and long-term sin problems are treated as reminders that we are "just human."
10. Remorse seems a sufficient step of repentance.
11. God's promises and reassurances are applied unconditionally.
12. The fight against evil becomes more a societal than a personal battle, especially in view of God's ultimate victory.
13. Self-examination seems a dangerous flirtation with guilt.
14. The "judgmental" label thwarts attempts to reprove and correct flagrant sin.
15. The Christian label may be broadly applied to those who serve the community or the church, or who express kindness, generosity, and pleasantness.

During Jesus' final evening with His disciples before His arrest and crucifixion, He spoke to them at length about the Promise, the Covenant, that would soon take effect: the coming of the Counselor, the Spirit of truth. The Holy Spirit had been present in the world since its beginning, of course. We read of His "hovering" over the surface of the waters as God prepared the earth to receive and support living beings.[6] God's Spirit had for centuries empowered men and women to believe God's promises, to worship God, to discern truth from error, to accomplish feats of valor—supernatural works at times—and to inspire God's servants and prophets to write down God's words for their own and future generations. However, His role was about to include something new, something better than before. Christ's atonement paved the way for a new era in God's relationship with humanity, a new stage in His unfolding plans, and the Holy Spirit was to play a central role in this new interaction.

One aspect of the Spirit's multifaceted role in this new Covenant was to remind the disciples of all Jesus' words and to lead and guide them (as well as all disciples to come after them) into greater understanding of truth, "all" truth. Jesus must have anticipated our difficulty in accepting some truth, truth that bothers us because we cannot see how it fits together in our familiar patterns of reasoning and problem solving. He anticipated our temptation to pick and choose pieces of truth to overlap other pieces when the puzzle's picture makes no sense to us. At such times, the Spirit can and will give us courage to face the whole truth squarely and to ask, as James says, for wisdom.

To understand and accept any key doctrine of the Christian faith requires an appeal to God's "higher ways" and "higher thoughts." Through the centuries Christians have struggled to force-fit the truth into a four-dimensional frame. Only by God's Spirit can we resist this compulsion that, as history and our own experience reveal, leads to strife, distortion, and division. Having seen the results of treating the dilemma over "Whose will holds sway?" as a contradiction, or as an antinomy, perhaps we are ready to discover what can be accomplished by approaching it as a paradox, or at least by putting it to the paradox test. We may still end up with truth we cannot picture in our mind's eye, but if we end up with a picture that makes sense, we will receive the benefits of embracing the whole truth rather than a lopsided portion of it.

Differing Frames of Reference
Chapter 6 lists steps that can be applied, singly or in combination, to identify and resolve paradoxes. If the approach works, we know we are dealing with a paradox rather than a contradiction. We have nothing to lose in applying these steps to the battle over wills. The first step is to identify the frame of reference for each of the truths under investigation. Differences here may cause or contribute to the clash. In the case of free will versus election, this step proves productive.

A review of the many Bible passages (see table 13.1, page 136) stating the truth of human free choice and the truth of divine predestination reveals this crucial distinction. Human (four-dimensional) perspective frames the statements affirming our freedom of choice and responsibility for our choices. Portions affirming God's sovereign control over all things, including human choice, are framed in the divine perspective that supersedes our natural realm, that is, that goes beyond our four dimensions.

In some passages, such as Joel 2:32 and 2 Corinthians 8:16-17, the two different perspectives appear together:

And everyone who calls on the name of the LORD will be saved; for on Mount Zion and in Jerusalem there will be deliverance, as the LORD has said, among the survivors whom the LORD calls.

I thank God, who put into the heart of Titus the same concern I have for you. For Titus not only welcomed our
appeal, but he is coming to you with much enthusiasm and
on his own initiative.

From the divine perspective, God calls or chooses those who
will be saved, while from our human perspective we do the calling
or choosing. Other verses declare just as clearly that no one receives
salvation without choosing to receive it, and that no one receives
salvation unless God chooses him or her to receive it. To state the
case another way, all humans who choose salvation will receive it,
and all humans whom God chooses to receive salvation will receive
it. In four-dimensional thinking, God's choosing makes us puppets
having no real freedom. Free choice for humans would be illusory
in light of this truth. But Scripture says otherwise. Somehow, trans-
ferring from one frame of reference to the other must help make
everything compatible. One does not cancel out the other.

The next step in paradox resolution calls for defining the sys-
tem(s) operating on each side of the question. The frame of reference suggests that on the human choice side, the system is defined
partly by humanity's space and time dimensions, but most importantly by the unidirectional, single time dimension in which cause
and effect always proceed in that order. Further, it is defined by limited freedom. Human life begins and unfolds with a number of
"givens" over which individuals have no choice. We cannot choose
to whom we are born, or when, or where, or how we will be treated
at different times by others. We cannot choose the characteristics of
body, mind, and personality that are genetically determined.
Absolute freedom of choice does not exist for human beings. God's
freedom of choice has limits, too, though His limits are self-
imposed, as described in chapter 12.

On the divine choice side, the system is defined by God's
dimensions, or their equivalent, which we know add up to at least
eleven, including more than one time dimension. Considering what
this extra-dimensionality makes possible, we begin to see how the
problem can be resolved; it does fit the definition of a paradox. The
system these verses reveal apparently allows human will and God's

will to operate independently in some contexts and interdependently in other contexts.

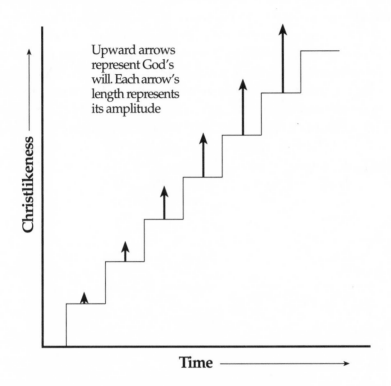

Figure 13.1: Increasing Influence of God's Will in Our Lives
Each step we take toward God, each decision to accept and act upon His light (that is, His love, life, and truth[7]) strengthens God's influence in our lives.

Schematic illustrations, as limited and oversimplified as they may be, help us grasp how such a system could operate. The system must include, of course, the influence of God's adversary, Satan, whose goal is to oppose God at every turn. As God draws us toward Himself, toward accepting His truth, life, and love, Satan, who instigated human rebellion, draws us away from God, tempting us to reject God's truth, life, and love. In such a system, every step we take toward God or away from Him has at least these three components: human choice, God's will, and the adversary's will. How God blends all three factors to carry out His plan we cannot definitively say, but a few of the options are presented at the end of this chapter.

Two of these components are predictable, at least in direction and in opposition to one another: God draws us to Himself, and Satan draws us away from Him. One component remains unpredictable from a human perspective: our choices to move toward God or away from Him. From our perspective, at least initially, our life is our own to do with as we choose, but somewhere along the way we become aware that to go our own way is tantamount to going Satan's way of self-exaltation. Relinquishing ourselves to that destiny amounts to refusing God's offer of everlasting life with Him. By the time our earthly life is over, every one of us, according to the Bible, will either become an adopted child of God[8] or a committed follower of a false god,[9] possibly our self.

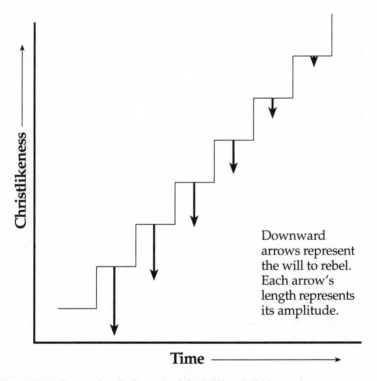

Downward arrows represent the will to rebel. Each arrow's length represents its amplitude.

Figure 13.2: Decreasing Influence of the Will to Rebel
Each step we take toward God, each decision to accept God's light, weakens the influence of God's adversary in our lives.

Each choice we make to believe and trust God, to bend our will to His, strengthens the influence of His will in our decision-making process.

In fact, we can observe these three effects, among others:

1. Each decision to move toward God (see figure 13.1, page 143) strengthens His influence on our next decision.
2. Each decision to move toward God weakens the temptation to move away from Him (see figure 13.2, page 144).
3. With each decision to move toward God, our character becomes more like Christ's[10] (see figures 13.1 and 13.2).

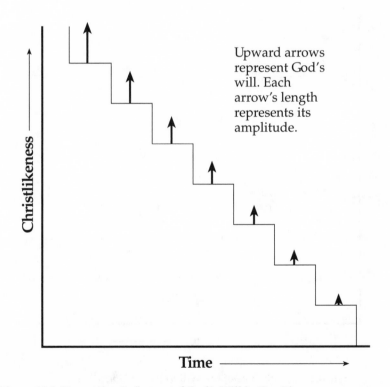

Figure 13.3: Decreasing Influence of God's Will in Our Lives

Each move we make away from God, each rejection of His light, results in a weakening of the tug in God's direction.

Conversely, as we go against God's will and reject His light, we experience the opposite results:

1. Each decision to reject God's light (see figure 13.3, page 145) weakens the tug in God's direction for our next decision.
2. Each decision to reject God's light increases the pull toward darkness (see figure 13.4, page 146).
3. With each decision to reject God's light, our character becomes less like Christ's and more like Satan's[11] (see figures 13.3 and 13.4).

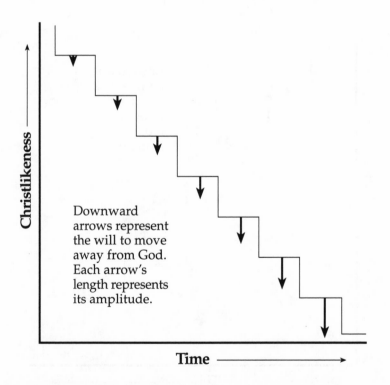

Figure 13.4: Increasing Influence of the Will to Reject God's Truth and Authority
Each move we make in opposition to God's will, each rejection of God's light, strengthens the pull in that direction for our next decision.

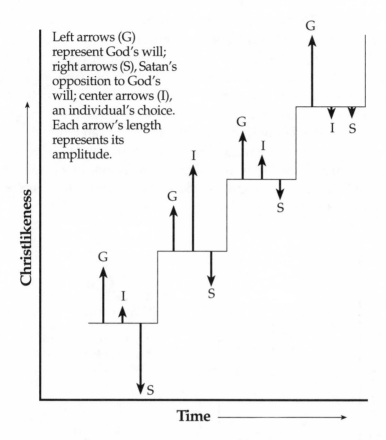

Left arrows (G) represent God's will; right arrows (S), Satan's opposition to God's will; center arrows (I), an individual's choice. Each arrow's length represents its amplitude.

Figure 13.5: Increasing Strength of God's Will Resulting from Choices to Obey
As choices to obey God strengthen the influence of God's will (**G**) in our lives, His will becomes strong enough to overpower ambivalence or a weak expression of rebellion (**I**).

The changing amplitude (expressed strength) of God's will, or influence, and of opposition to it by His adversary's will, or influence, seems generally predictable, at least in a relative sense, and is consistent. The same cannot be said about the operation of our own will. The strength (or weakness) with which we express our will in either direction is up to us. For as long as we live and for as many decisions as we make to move in God's direction or away, the strength with which we express our will remains variable. We can exercise it strongly or weakly at virtually any point along the way.

As figure 13.5 (page 147) suggests, a pattern of movement toward God, of accepting His truth and authority, brings a bonus benefit. People whose lives manifest such a pattern can testify that at moments when they faltered in their decision to obey God and even expressed mild resistance, they ended up obeying in spite of themselves. Figure 13.6 suggests that the reverse may also occur. People with a long record of movement away from God can testify that in moments when they are weakly inclined to choose in His direction, they end up rejecting His truth and authority, in spite of themselves. Repeated acceptance strengthens God's influence; repeated rejection strengthens the influence of His adversary.

Left arrows (G) represent God's will; right arrows (S), Satan's opposition to God's will; center arrows (I), an individual's choice. Each arrow's length represents its amplitude.

Figure 13.6: Increasing Strength of the Will to Rebel Resulting from Choices to Disobey
As choices to reject God's truth and authority weaken the influence of God's will (**G**) in our lives and strengthen the tug of rebellion, the will to rebel (**I**) becomes strong enough to overpower ambivalence or a weak choice to obey.

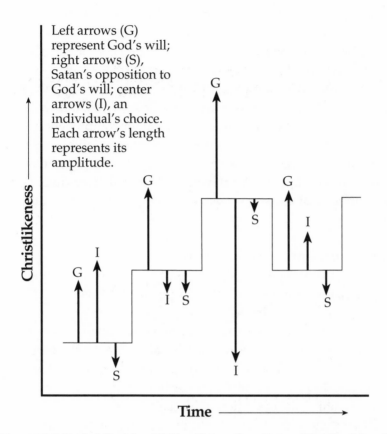

Figure 13.7: Typical Decision-Making Pattern for a Person Who Has Moved Gradually Toward God
Strong expression of disobedience or rejection still can move this person away from God. But, because God's influence (**G**) has become so much stronger than what it was and Satan's (**S**) so much weaker, if the person merely expresses his or her individual will (**I**) as before, he or she will be drawn to God much more powerfully than before.

No human being always obeys and accepts God's way or always opposes His way. Each person does some accepting and some rejecting, some trusting and some distrusting, some obeying and some disobeying. Figure 13.7 depicts the typical choice pattern a person might manifest during and after a period of movement toward Christ. Figures could also be designed to depict a choice pattern after a net movement away from Christ, or a period of wavering back and forth in the middle. In the next chapter we will take a look at where this decision-making process leads: to the unavoidable crossing of the line in God's direction or Satan's during our lifetime—long or short—here on Earth.

What we have done here is to expose the dynamics of the seeming clash of truths about our will and God's will. And while an understanding of these dynamics is critical for comprehending the resolution of the paradox, it is not sufficient to complete the resolution. But we already know we need to apply step eight from the list in chapter 6 (see page 54), namely to calculate or discern the effects of dimensions or realms in which human measurements cannot be made.

God's Cause and Effect Capacities

We have looked in previous chapters at God's amazing capacities within two time dimensions or their equivalent. We saw how God's operation in an extra time dimension or two can help make sense of His capacities to hear everyone's prayers simultaneously and to atone for humanity's sin in one sacrificial act. We can also discern that a three-dimensional time domain or its equivalent would enable God to predetermine every action of every human being while sustaining the operation of human choice.

Three-dimensional time could be depicted, for example, as a sphere with lines of time running parallel to the equator (latitudes), perpendicular to the equator (longitudes), and from the center, or other interior points, out to the surface and beyond (radials). The time line of the universe, with us on it, could be placed along a particular latitude of this sphere.

For purposes of demonstration, let's return to the figure of a three-dimensional time sphere introduced in chapter 6. Let's put the universe's time line along the 30-degree latitude north. While our experience of time would be limited to advancing forward along that latitude, God could operate from anywhere along, within, or exterior to the surface of the time sphere. He could, for example, position Himself at the north pole of the sphere. From that single time point, He could drop a time line perpendicular to our date of birth, to the moment of our present existence, to the instant of our physical death, to the beginning of the physical universe or before, and to the moment when He replaces this universe with a new one (see figure 13.8). Any and all of these perpendicular time lines meet together at a single point. This convergence implies that God can impact events throughout the history of the universe and the course of our lives (and more) in a single instant of His time.

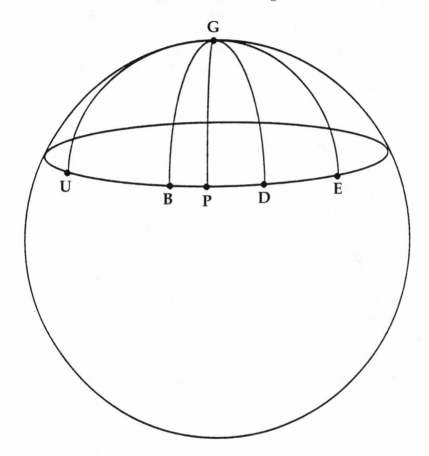

Figure 13.8: God's Operations in a Sphere of Time
In three dimensions of time or the equivalent, God could generate causes anywhere within, on, or outside the sphere. The line segment **UE** represents the time dimension of the universe. At point **U** the universe comes into existence. At point **E** its existence ends. **B** is the birth date for an individual human. **D** is his or her time of death, and **P** the present moment. God, from a single point or instant of time, say **G**, could simultaneously influence points **U, B, P, D**, and **E** along our time line.

In two time dimensions, infinite time on our time line can be shrunk down to less than a trillionth of a second for God (see chapter 7, pages 62-63). Adding a third time dimension allows for infinite time to the infinite power (that is, ∞) to be compressed into less than a trillionth of a second. Billions of years in our time dimension and much, much more can be just a single instant for God.

In that single instant, God could see every event in all time, including every event in the lives of every human being who has ever lived, is living, or ever will live. He would see in exquisite detail everything that belongs to our future. The past and future are the present for Him. As Jesus said,

> "I am the Alpha and Omega, the First and the Last, the Beginning and the End."[12]

Scripture affirms that He does indeed possess these unique attributes and capacities. His foreknowledge[13] and His identity as "I AM"[14] receive no debate from either Arminians or Calvinists.

Because of God's power and love, His foreknowledge implies much more than mere possession of information. He has the capacity to use that information to influence future events. In his letter to the Romans Paul says, "For those God foreknew he also predestined to be conformed to the likeness of his Son."[15] In the ninth chapter he adds,

> Yet, before the twins [Jacob and Esau] were born or had done anything good or bad—in order that God's purpose in election might stand: not by works but by him who calls—she [Rebekah, their mother] was told, "The older will serve the younger." Just as it is written: "Jacob I loved, but Esau I hated."[16]

And in the eleventh chapter we read,

> God did not reject his people, whom he foreknew. . . . At the present time there is a remnant chosen by grace.[17]

Peter begins a letter to fellow believers with these words:

> To God's elect . . . who have been chosen according to the foreknowledge of God the Father, through the sanctifying work of the Spirit, for obedience to Jesus Christ and sprinkling by his blood.[18]

In three or more dimensions of time or the equivalent, God's foreknowing and predestining can be one and the same. As figure 13.8 (page 151) shows, God has the capacity to view every event along our time line from a single instant and, from that same instant, to generate cause and effect phenomena anywhere along that time line. God can in a moment of His time cause events to happen before, during, and after the sixteen-billion-year history of the universe.[19] Literally, from before the universe even existed, from before our dimension of time even existed, God had access to every event in the history of the cosmos and every action, word, and thought that every human being would ever experience throughout his or her life.

Predestined and Free

The crucial question remains: How does God do the predestining while guaranteeing us the freedom of our will, as the Scriptures and our understanding of love demand? How does God predetermine every choice without infringing on our control over the human choice vectors depicted in the previous figures? Several workable ways are made possible by the existence of His extra-dimensional powers. Here are two:

Resolution one: God can see not only what occurs throughout a person's life but also the events and conditions (physically, mentally, emotionally, and spiritually) in which things occur. Each of us expresses our will in response to complex internal and external factors. Knowing all these factors, including the characteristics of our personality, the effects of our experiences and communications with people and even with angels and demons, God anticipates the direction of each choice and how strongly we will express our will in any instance. Thus, God could prescribe the exact conditions to generate the response of our will at any given moment that fits into His total plan. We would remain continuously in control of our will, while God would continuously control the circumstances and conditions in and around us that impact our will.

Resolution two: Let's assume two precepts are true: (1) Every step we make toward God, every acceptance and trust of His truth, strengthens His influence in our lives and weakens the influence of His adversary to encourage us to reject Him; and (2) every step of rejection weakens the influence of God's will while strengthening His adversary's influence on us to rebel against His authority. Then God can determine at each point of decision what amplitude of His will and Satan's will brings about the net response that fits into His total plan. In this scenario, we would remain continuously in control of our will while God would remain continuously in control of all the increases and decreases of the effects of His will, as well as of Satan's will, on each one of us.

A slight revision of this resolution scenario would call for God to increase or decrease to whatever degree at whatever time the amplitude of any or all of the three choice vectors. The individual would still be free to exercise his or her will, but whatever influence the individual (or God or Satan) exerts could be amplified or diminished by whatever amount God sees necessary to His total plan.

Given the many, perhaps infinitely, more dimensions or their equivalent available to God, many more resolutions, perhaps infinitely more and better ones, could be offered that preserve the freedom of human choice (control over the central vector in figures 13.5 to 13.7) while acknowledging God's sovereign control over all His creation and beyond.

One reason for proposing these two possible resolutions (plus a variation) centers on the importance of biblical revelation as a reality check. These two scenarios seem consistent, as far as we can tell, with the relevant Scripture passages citing one or both sides of the paradox. The Bible records God's use of natural elements to influence the affairs of humanity.[20] It also attests to God's use of supernatural elements to influence the affairs of humanity.[21] Isaiah, Daniel, and Jude personally experienced dramatic examples of such supernatural occurrences and wrote extensively about their influence in Scripture. The Bible also promises that we will not be tempted above what we are able to bear.[22]

Both scenarios, as well as a combination of the two, seem to be biblically possible. As to which is more biblically favored, at this point much more theological, philosophical, and scientific research appears necessary to render anything more than an educated guess or preference.

The bottom line is that we cannot expect to be able to form an adequate picture in our minds of how human choice and divine choice can both be fully operational, but if we accept both truths because the Bible teaches them and because God's extra-dimensional powers demonstrate the possibility of making sense of them, we can experience both the challenge and comfort we need to live as God's children. We need the challenge of responsibility for our choices, and we also need the comfort of comprehending, even to a limited degree, how all things, including our unwise choices and others' choices that impact our lives, can work together for good, for the accomplishment of God's ultimate purpose and plan.[23]

So far, we have examined only the paradox of the freedom of human choice and the sovereignty of God's will from the standpoint of someone not yet fully committed to God's camp or to Satan's camp. Of greater concern to most people is an understanding of the impact of this paradox on the end of their lives here on Earth as compared to the beginning or the middle. Thus, no resolution of this paradox would be complete or humanly satisfying without also looking into this important corollary.

CHAPTER FOURTEEN

EXTRA-DIMENSIONALITY AND SALVATION'S SECURITY

How does the decision-making process, schematically illustrated in the previous chapter, lead to crossing the commitment line—what some have termed points of no return, either in God's direction or in Satan's? The answer to that question is best understood if we first complete the paradox resolution steps regarding God's will and the wills of human beings.

What is the interplay between the two wills in deciding who will be God's and who will not? Because we traditionally have approached the question of wills as something other than a paradox, emphasizing either the prevalence of human choice or the prevalence of God's, further divisions have arisen among individuals and churches over this corollary question: Is our salvation a sure thing, a matter of "once saved, always saved," or can we lose it, either by lack of vigilance or by deliberate choice?

Intents of the Heart

Each of us who are believers brings our personal concerns and emotions about family members and friends that tend to cloud the issue. Most Christians have known at least one person who professed faith in Jesus Christ; attended church; took communion; read the Bible; was baptized in water; served in the church as a choir member, Sunday school teacher, usher, deacon, or other leader; perhaps even attended Bible college or seminary and entered the pastorate—but who at some point turned away from Christ and lived as anything but a Christian. Is this individual guaranteed eternal life with God?

157

What about the millions of people in culturally Christian nations who live for their own pleasure, have no connection with any Christian fellowship, and yet claim they are born again and heaven bound?

We wonder about such things because we resemble, in one sense, the computer screen people. We see each others' outsides, and the outsides do give us some important clues to what goes on inside. But we lack God's extra-dimensional perspective to look directly upon the "thoughts and intents of the heart." So we are fundamentally ignorant. While God can handle such intimate knowledge, evidently we in our present state cannot.

The underlying question we need to consider is this: How is anyone "saved"? According to Scripture, salvation comes by choice—both ours *and* God's, not by one or the other. If we emphasize our choice over God's, we may take too much responsibility for our salvation and worry about keeping or losing it; while we do not know our future circumstances, we do know our will is sometimes weak and often changeable. If we emphasize God's choice over ours, we may lean so heavily on His will that we take too little responsibility for our spiritual life, never even bothering to check our hearts to see if we are walking in faith or in presumption.[1]

Initial and Final Conditions

To find and maintain a better balance on this important issue, let us apply step three from the list in chapter 6 (see page 54) to the paradox of the wills: Identify correctly and completely the initial conditions and final conditions of the phenomenon (or phenomena) under investigation. Initial conditions and final conditions must be connected to a time line, in this case, the universe's time line. God, as the Bible explains, is immutable,[2] and He is not confined to a single time line. So His "conditions" remain unchanged.

Initial conditions for humanity, with respect to free choice and salvation, include the following:

1. God placed immortal spirit in an earthly body, male and female, endowed with the freedom to enjoy a relationship of honor and worship toward Him. As long as these

first humans remained untested, they remained in that wondrous state of innocence; yet not as puppets, but with the real potential to shatter both their innocence and their relationship with God.

2. The Tempter, Satan—once the highest of God's angelic creation, now the proud adversary—provided the ultimate test of these humans' mettle. If they chose to resist whatever temptation(s) he could muster, they would prove their capacity to withstand any test of their will to honor God's authority and to retain their innocence. However, each of their offspring would face the same test to serve God or not based on his or her own free choice.

Scripture records how well Adam and Eve did. They eliminated all suspense by falling into the very first temptation Satan offered. But their fall is just the beginning of the story. In fact, it is a step in the direction of the final conditions described for us in the book of Revelation, as well as in other parts of Scripture:

1. God will place our spirits in indestructible bodies fit for existence in dimensions beyond earth's four, no longer bound by the laws and limits of earthly existence.
2. We humans will enjoy a relationship—side by side with the angelic hosts—of honor and worship toward God, freely chosen and tested under the toughest possible conditions and thus no longer subject to shattering. Or, we will receive the outcome of our choice to reject that relationship, despite ample opportunities to say yes, and will share eternity with all those who also have refused it, including Satan and his cohorts, the demons (or fallen angels).

When the universe's time line ends, we come to a great divide. No longer will believers and unbelievers, angels and demons, the Prince of Peace and the prince of horrors, interact with one another. Though our will can still be expressed (the angels' too), its direction is fixed like the arrow of a compass, and nothing in us or around us can sway us from our course.

But these final conditions, which we will explore in the context of human beings in chapters 16 and 17, remain for the future. The course of events by which they are attained is still unfolding, as it has been since before the beginning of the world. We read a history of the highlights in the pages of the Bible:

1. God was prepared for the Fall in the Garden of Eden. He planned that through the physical death of humans, the extent of their sin could be held in check.
2. He promised to deliver from all sin those who choose to be delivered.
3. He prompted faith in that promised deliverance through the giving of the Law.
4. Through Christ, the sinless "Adam," God paid the death penalty for humanity's sin and graciously provided an inheritance of eternal life in communion with Him.
5. Christ sent the Holy Spirit to "seal" the promise, securely grafting all who choose eternal life with God into the Vine (see John 15:1-17), filling them with both the desire and the power to do His will.
6. The Holy Spirit empowers those in whom He lives to participate in preparation for the new creation, especially by becoming living invitations for other people to join in this new life.

We read about the movement from initial conditions to final conditions on the universe's time line in God's Word and in history's annals. The one part of that process we directly observe transpires in our own life spans. For each of us, earthly life begins with sin's penalty over our heads, as well as God's pardon extended to us. No one but God knows what we, or others around us, will do with that pardon—seize it or toss it aside. By life's end, even if no one else knows, God sees what we have done with it.

No one leaves this life in the middle ground between eternal connection with God and eternal separation from Him. And no one stumbles into that connection or separation without knowing what he or she is choosing. As Paul declares in Romans 1:20-21, no one has an excuse for worshiping anyone or anything but the Creator of heaven and earth. Knowledge of His existence, His identity, His qualities, His justice, His mercy and His power have been made understandable to all.[3]

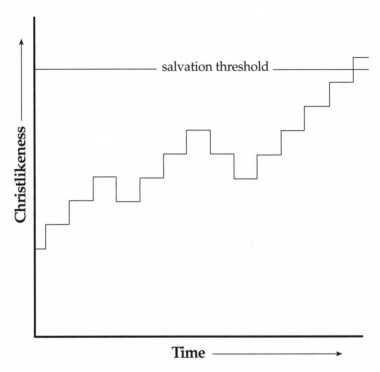

Figure 14.1: Journey Toward Salvation
The steps up depict choices to accept God's love, life, and truth, while the steps down depict choices to reject God's love, life, and truth. The process of becoming Christlike is not to be interpreted as the accumulation of good works but rather the development of humility, submission, and godly character.

Approaching the Salvation Threshold
We humans tend to hear a lot of excuses and see many people whose choices never become clear to us before their deaths. The problem, once again, is that we lack God's extra-dimensional vision. To find further answers to our questions, we can apply step four from the paradox resolution list: Gather more information on the circumstances surrounding the phenomenon in question.

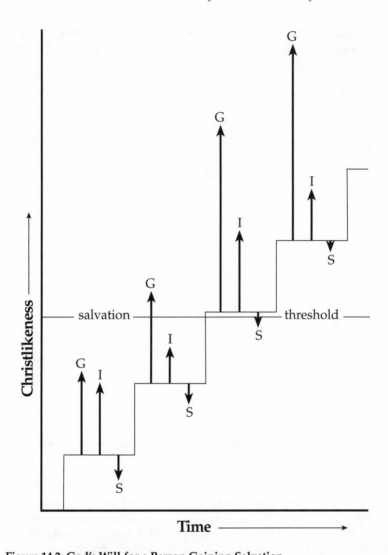

Figure 14.2: God's Will for a Person Gaining Salvation
As one approaches or advances beyond the salvation threshold, God's will (**G**) in one's life gets stronger in small increments. Crossing the threshold, however, results in a substantial increase in God's will in one's life. Meanwhile, Satan's will (**S**) continues to gradually decrease, but the individual retains the freedom to express his or her own will (**I**).

Figure 14.1 (page 161) offers another schematic illustration of the decision-making process in the life of a person proceeding toward salvation. As the figure reminds us, the journey toward salvation usually proceeds along a bumpy, up-and-down path. At times we accept and follow God's way, and at times we resist and rebel against it. But the closer we draw to the salvation threshold, the greater the probability that downward dips will decrease in number and magnitude. As figures 13.1 to 13.7 indicate, the more we say yes to God's truth, the more like Christ we become and the stronger the influence of God's will in our lives. At the same time, the capacity for Satan to influence us to rebel against God grows weaker.

Changes at the Line Crossing

When we cross over the line by surrendering ourselves—our past, present, and future—to God, exchanging our best and worst efforts for His gracious gift, His Holy Spirit enters our being. (See figure 14.2 on page 162.) We gain access to His strength for living in the Light, and His fruit begins to grow in us.[4]

We do not then begin a life of perfect obedience. We still wrestle with doubt, cowardice, selfishness, and other wrong actions, attitudes, and choices. We still sometimes take detours around God's ways in seeking to meet our needs and wants. When we move in the wrong direction, though, He allows us to experience sometimes painful consequences to guide us back in the right direction. And when we move in His direction, even when doing so is occasionally terribly painful to our body and soul, He rewards us with peace, joy, and affirmation. When trials and tragedies strike, we may be staggered for a while, lost in our hurt, anger, and confusion. When success strikes, we may be staggered for a while, lost in our self-satisfaction and pride. But His influence remains. His faith holds us. We can count on His capacity, not on our own, to keep us from falling below that crucial line.[5]

The One-Way Crossing

Or can we? As I have indicated above, believers have differing views on whether the salvation line can be crossed two ways, not only *into* salvation's territory but *out* again. The confusion arises not only from experience with people, but also from certain portions of Scripture. Table 14.1 (page 164) provides a fairly comprehensive list of the Bible verses addressing salvation's security.

Table 14.1: Bible Verses Concerning Whether or Not Believers Can Lose Their Salvation

1 Sam. 2:8-9	John 11:25-26	2 Tim. 1:9
Job 1:8-11	John 14:16	2 Tim. 1:12
Job 17:9	John 15:6	2 Tim. 2:17-19
Job 23:10	John 17:12	2 Tim. 4:18
Ps. 34:19	John 18:9	Heb. 2:14-15
Ps. 37:28	Acts 27:21-44	Heb. 3:6
Ps. 66:9	Rom. 5:10	Heb. 3:14-19
Ps. 68:18	Rom. 6:2-11	Heb. 4:11
Ps. 73:23-28	Rom. 6:14	Heb. 6:4-9
Ps. 87:5-6	Rom. 6:23	Heb. 6:17-19
Ps. 89:32-33	Rom. 7:14–8:17	Heb. 7:25
Ps. 138:8	Rom. 8:27-29	Heb. 8:12
Prov. 12:3	Rom. 8:35-39	Heb. 9:12
Prov. 18:10	Rom. 11:1-33	Heb. 10:14
Prov. 29:1	Rom. 13:11	Heb. 10:17
Eccl. 3:14	1 Cor. 6:19	Heb. 10:26-39
Song 8:7	1 Cor. 8:11	Heb. 13:5-6
Is. 14:27	1 Cor. 9:27	Heb. 13:21
Jer. 31:3	1 Cor. 10:12-14	James 1:22-25
Jer. 32:40	1 Cor. 12:13	1 Peter 1:3-9
Ezek. 18:20-32	1 Cor. 15:2	1 Peter 5:6-10
Ezek. 34:15-16	1 Cor. 15:51	2 Peter 1:10
Dan. 9:24	2 Cor. 1:21-22	2 Peter 2:20-22
Hos. 6:4	2 Cor. 3:7-11	2 Peter 3:17
Hos. 14:1-5	2 Cor. 5:5	1 John 1:5-10
Mal. 3:6	2 Cor. 6:1	1 John 2:19
Matt. 7:21-23	2 Cor. 7:1	1 John 2:27-28
Matt. 13:1-23	2 Cor. 12:9	1 John 3:1-2
Matt. 16:18	Gal. 5:4-6	1 John 4:18
Matt. 18:23-35	Eph. 1:5	1 John 5:11-13
Matt. 25:1-13	Eph. 1:13-14	1 John 5:18
Mark 12:32-34	Eph. 2:10	2 John 8
Mark 13:22	Eph. 4:30	Jude 1
Luke 8:13	Phil. 1:6	Jude 12
Luke 10:20	Phil. 2:12-13	Jude 24
John 6:39	Col. 1:22-23	Rev. 2:5
John 6:66	Col. 2:12-15	Rev. 3:11
John 10:27-29	1 Tim. 1:19	

The verses most often cited as proof that salvation can be found and then lost include Hebrews 6:4-6, 10:26-31, and 2 Peter 2:20-22. These passages do not suggest that we human beings have the propensity to cross the line back and forth, into and out of salvation.

Rather, they say that a person who understands what God is offering, including who is offering and the benefits of accepting, and still chooses to "trample on" that offer, will never experience a change of heart. Salvation rejected by such an individual remains lost forever. The crucial question is whether this individual can rightly be considered a Christian in the first place. Some argue that the description can apply to a believer.

A closer look at both the text and the context suggests another possibility. This closer look at the text's words, their meaning and context, approximates step five from the list of paradox resolution methods: Make more precise measurements. Though we cannot "measure" words as we would typical research data, this step toward more precise interpretation accomplishes a similar goal.

The Hebrews 6 passage describes those "who have tasted the heavenly gift, who have shared in the Holy Spirit, who have tasted the goodness of the word of God and the powers of the coming age." Hebrews 10:26 identifies these individuals as having "knowledge of the truth." And 2 Peter 2:20-21 describes them as "knowing our Lord and Savior Jesus Christ" and knowing "the way of righteousness." All of these descriptive phrases could apply to Christians; but must they, necessarily?

All the qualifying clauses and phrases in Hebrews and 2 Peter seem to constitute the necessary steps for coming to Christ, but they do not clearly imply that the all-important salvation transaction has been made. In other words, the individuals to whom these passages refer have come to understand and acknowledge everything they need to know to enter a relationship with God, but they may not have stepped across salvation's threshold in repentance, acceptance of God's forgiveness, and surrender to God's authority.

The English phrase "have shared in the Holy Spirit" may seem the clearest reference to Christians. Yet Kenneth S. Wuest and Arthur W. Pink, among other scholars, explain that the Greek word translated "shared in," *metochos*, denotes something less than possession of (or by) the Holy Spirit. More accurately it suggests that these people have received certain benefits and blessings from the Holy Spirit, a taste of what He is like.[6-7]

The definitive statements identifying the subjects of the Hebrews and 2 Peter passages come after the cautionary words. Many interpreters stop reading before they come to them, but they belong to the context and cannot be overlooked. Hebrews 6:9 says, "Even though we speak like this, dear friends, we are confident of better things in your case—things that accompany salvation." Hebrews 10:39 concludes with this assurance: "But we are not of those who shrink back and are destroyed, but of those who believe and are saved."

Peter finishes with metaphors that no first-century reader would mistake for a reference to a child of God: "A dog returns to its vomit," and "A sow that is washed goes back to her wallowing in the mud."[8] To first-century Jews, only God-rejecting unbelievers could be referred to with such derogatory terms as dogs and pigs.

These passages, then, must refer to people who, like the Pharisees, have known who Jesus is and what He offers and yet have decided in their hearts, "We will not have this man [Jesus] to rule over us!"

Additional evidence comes from the other side of the question, the side that says a person who is placed in Christ by the Spirit and in whom Christ places the Spirit can never be plucked out, not even by his own words and actions. As Paul declares in Romans:

> For I am convinced that neither death nor life, neither
> angels nor demons, neither the present nor the future, nor
> any powers, neither height nor depth, nor anything else in
> all creation, will be able to separate us from the love of God
> that is in Christ Jesus our Lord.[9]

This passage seems to leave no loopholes, no qualifying phrase, such as "except a person's decision to reject the love of God." Moreover, three other Bible passages state that when an individual truly makes a commitment of his or her life to Jesus Christ, from that moment onward, he or she receives a guarantee of entry into heaven and of eternal life with God.[10]

Why Warnings About Loss?

The Hebrews and 2 Peter passages represent just a few of the many Bible verses warning unbelievers against loss. Additional warnings, unquestionably aimed at believers, seem unsettling to the case for salvation's security, however strong its supporting Scriptures may appear. Believers are given these exhortations:

> Continue to work out your salvation with fear and trembling.[11]

> Be on your guard so that you may not be carried away by the error of lawless men and fall from your secure position.[12]

> Watch out that you do not lose what you have worked for, but that you may be rewarded fully.[13]

When we see the words "worked for," we discover an important clue that the passage refers to something other than salvation's free gift, which no "work" of ours can ever possibly merit.[14] The solution to this aspect of the paradox lies in the distinction of salvation's three meanings or stages. Bible scholars have for centuries recognized that salvation's threshold is "justification"—complete deliverance from sin's penalty, received the moment a person becomes joined to God through Christ. Salvation's ongoing "work" is called "sanctification"—our walk in the Light, through which we discover and express greater and greater freedom from our ungodly ways of thinking and living. "Glorification" may be glimpsed in moments now, as God reveals Himself to others through us; but it remains as our promise of total and permanent freedom from sin as we are received into Christ's glorified presence, the place He is preparing for us.

The apostles' warnings aptly apply to believers who may be tempted to twist God's grace, confusing the freedom not to sin for the freedom to sin without penalty or loss. We can lose ground in our growth toward Christlikeness, and that loss can be painfully serious. According to 1 Corinthians 3, our Christian life can be built with gold, silver, and gems, or it can be built with wood, hay, and straw. Verses 13-15 present this picture:

The fire will test the quality of each man's work. If what he has built survives, he will receive his reward. If it is burned up, he will suffer loss; he himself will be saved, but only as one escaping through the flames.

The blessing to be gained by cooperating with God, exercising our will in the direction of the upward arrows in the schematic illustration, will be greater by far, both in this life and beyond, than any of us can possibly imagine.

Salvation's Counterpart

As I have mentioned, no one ends earthly life in the middle ground between life and death, connection and separation. We know from Jesus' words and from the Hebrews passages cited above that a sin can be committed for which no forgiveness remains, no possibility of turning back. We have been instructed to offer no prayers for those who have crossed that line,[15] a line that may be described as the counterpart to the salvation line. Scripture calls it "blasphemy against the Holy Spirit."

Misunderstanding of this condemnation threshold has caused anguish to many believers. Because it is often termed "the unpardonable sin," people imagine it is a one-time blunder for which they will be forever damned. Instead, blasphemy appears to be the result of many choices to reject God's light, including His authority. The progression toward blasphemy can be seen in biblical narratives, such as the account of Egypt's pharaoh, who repeatedly and knowingly hardened his heart toward the Almighty until he passed a point of no return.[16-17]

The first use of the specific expression, "blasphemy against the Holy Spirit," appears in the New Testament. Mark quotes Jesus as saying:

"I tell you the truth, all the sins and blasphemies of men will be forgiven them. But whoever blasphemes against the Holy Spirit will never be forgiven; he is guilty of an eternal sin."[18]

Table 14.2 gives a comprehensive list of relevant Scripture passages. A study and integration of those verses leads to a composite

**Table 14.2: Bible Verses Concerning Blasphemy
Against the Holy Spirit**

Gen. 6:5	Is. 48:6-8,22	John 5:39-40,44-47
Ex. 7:14	Is. 56:10-12	John 6:36
Deut. 28:20	Is. 65:12	John 7:32
1 Sam. 15:23	Jer. 6:10,16-17	John 8:24-27,33
2 Chr. 36:16	Jer. 7:13-28	John 8:37-38,40,43-49
Ps. 10:3-11	Jer. 9:5-6	John 9:16-34,39-41
Ps. 14:1	Jer. 11:8	John 10:24-26
Ps. 36:1-4	Jer. 17:5,23	John 11:47-48
Ps. 53:1	Jer. 18:12	John 12:9-10
Ps. 64:5-6	Jer. 44:16-18	John 18:4-9,38
Ps. 73:6-12	Hos. 4:16-18	Acts 7:42
Ps. 81:11-12	Hos. 5:3-7	Acts 17:21
Ps. 106:24	Amos 5:10	Acts 24:22-27
Ps. 107:11	Zeph. 3:5	Rom. 1:18-32
Prov. 1:7	Zech. 7:11-12	Rom. 8:1
Prov. 1:24-31	Mal. 2:17	1 Cor. 1:18
Prov. 2:12-15	Matt. 2:16	Gal. 1:7-9
Prov. 5:12-13	Matt. 5:11	Eph. 4:19
Prov. 9:7	Matt. 9:33-34	2 Thes. 2:8-12
Prov. 12:15-16	Matt. 10:25	1 Tim. 1:3-7
Prov. 14:6,9	Matt. 11:16-21	1 Tim. 4:1-3
Prov. 15:5,12	Matt. 12:7,13-14	2 Tim. 3:1-9
Prov. 17:15,24	Matt. 12:22-35	2 Tim. 4:2-5
Prov. 18:2	Matt. 13:14-15	Titus 1:15-16
Prov. 19:3	Matt. 21:14-16,32-46	Titus 3:9-11
Prov. 21:24	Matt. 22:1-6,15-17	Heb. 6:4-9
Prov. 23:9	Matt. 23:13-15	Heb. 10:26-31
Prov. 26:4-12	Matt. 24:10,38-39	Heb. 12:15-17
Prov. 27:22	Matt. 24:48-51	2 Pet. 2:1-22
Prov. 29:1	Matt. 26:63-68	2 Pet. 3:3-4
Prov. 30:12	Matt. 27:25	1 John 5:16-17
Eccl. 10:12-15	Matt. 28:11-14	2 John 10
Is. 1:4	Mark 3:22-30	Jude 4,8,10
Is. 3:9	Mark 11:18	Jude 12-13,16,18
Is. 5:12,18-24	Luke 6:22	Rev. 2:20
Is. 6:9-10	Luke 7:30-35	Rev. 3:3,17
Is. 10:13	Luke 12:10	Rev. 9:20-21
Is. 22:12-14	Luke 13:14-16	Rev. 16:9,21
Is. 29:13	Luke 16:27-31	Rev. 22:11
Is. 30:9-11	Luke 22:67-71	
Is. 42:20	John 3:18-19	

picture of the blasphemer. This individual knowingly and repeatedly defies God, rejecting His offer of forgiveness and eternal fellowship, rejecting all the Holy Spirit's promptings toward humility
and submission to God's truth and grace.

A schematic illustration of an individual's descent toward blasphemy against the Holy Spirit appears in figure 14.3. Though at
times this individual does right and responds in the direction of
God's will, the closer the rejecter gets to the blasphemy threshold,
the greater the probability that rebellion against God's authority
and rejection of God's light will become more frequent and more
strongly expressed.

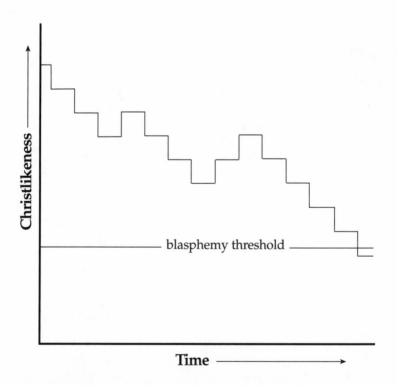

Figure 14.3: Journey Toward Blaspheming the Holy Spirit
The steps down depict acts of rebellion against God's authority or acts of rejecting God's love, life, and truth while the steps up depict acts of obedience or acts
of accepting God's love, life, and truth.

As the pattern of ongoing animosity toward God continues, eventually it will drive this person across the blasphemy threshold. There, the will of God in the person's life becomes so weak and the will of Satan so strong that the probability of his or her ever rising above the blasphemy threshold drops to zero. This individual has willingly and permanently entered Satan's camp.

Blasphemers cross over when God finally "gives them over" to their own sinfulness and rebellion. In the first chapter of Romans Paul uses these words to describe what happens to people who purposely "suppress the truth by their wickedness":

God gave them over in the sinful desires of their hearts to sexual impurity for the degrading of their bodies with one another.[19]

God gave them over to shameful lusts.[20]

He gave them over to a depraved mind, to do what ought not to be done.[21]

These and other verses indicate that at the moment anyone drops below the blasphemy threshold, the strength of God's influence in that person's life drops sharply (see figure 14.4, page 172). As the rebellion in a person's heart becomes fixed, God gives that individual what he or she has been longing for. He literally gives that person up to his or her own, and Satan's, ways.

Disproportionate Numbers

We may wonder why, if this inward progression toward salvation and blasphemy is going on in the lives of people throughout history and all around us today, the believers seem to outnumber by far the committed blasphemers, who are given over to depravity. One explanation may be that God's love works to extend the lives of those who are coming to salvation and to shorten the lives of those guaranteed condemnation.

God's desire is to maximize the eternal rewards of believers. Thus, God's love works to give each believer the necessary time to complete the good works He has prepared in advance for him or her to do.[22] It also works to give them ample time to become mature, to grow in developing the character attributes of Christ.[23]

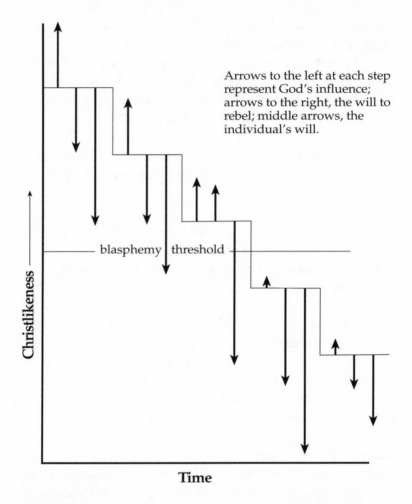

Arrows to the left at each step represent God's influence; arrows to the right, the will to rebel; middle arrows, the individual's will.

blasphemy | threshold

Christlikeness

Time

Figure 14.4: Blasphemy's Effect on God's Influence in a Person's Life
As an individual moves toward the blasphemy threshold, the tug of God lessens. Crossing the threshold results in a substantial decrease, perhaps a total loss. Meanwhile, Satan's influence increases and the individual's freedom to express his or her own will remains the same.

God's love is at work as well to limit the evil and suffering that the blasphemers will bring about, both to themselves and to others.[24] Typically, the longer God allows such persons to live, the greater judgments they would pile up against themselves.[25] Thus, in many if not most cases, unredeemable reprobates die soon after crossing the blasphemy threshold.

Difficult to Discern

Much of the dispute among Christians over the doctrines of eternal security and blasphemy against the Holy Spirit stems from our human inability to discern exactly when a particular individual crosses either the threshold of salvation or the threshold of blasphemy. Sometimes that crossover seems abundantly clear, but even in such cases we can be wrong.

Few of us have encountered an actual blasphemer, though we may have met many people apparently moving in the direction of blasphemy. Moreover, since Satan's influence is so destructive, the farther below the blasphemy threshold a person goes, the more likely he or she is to self-destruct or to meet death at the hands of evil companions.

Since Christians are more numerous in our population than blasphemers against the Holy Spirit, we might assume we could more easily distinguish who has crossed salvation's threshold and who has not. However, that line is blurred, as I mentioned above, by our limited perspective and, thus, by our tendency to make hasty and superficial evaluations. Individuals and churches differ widely on what they consider the evidences of the indwelling Holy Spirit, by whom our salvation is secured. Many people who appear to us to be Christians meet about as many of the actual criteria for faith as did the Pharisees and Sadducees—and we know how they, with rare exceptions, responded to Jesus in their hearts. Jesus said that they never belonged to God.[26]

God alone knows, at any given moment, exactly where each of us stands on the Christlikeness scale. But, because our capacity to discern is so limited, we must proceed cautiously in expressing absolute certainty that a person is "in Christ." We know He will keep whatever we commit to Him,[27] but justification occurs when we yield to Him His right to rule our whole being, including the parts we have hidden from ourselves.

Dependent Paradoxes

As this chapter demonstrates, many biblical paradoxes encompass or intersect other paradoxes. Some of these paradoxes cannot be resolved satisfactorily without first resolving or demonstrating the resolvability of more fundamental paradoxes. As we have seen, many questions concerning the security of our salvation and on what it rests could only be answered by more complete resolution of deeper-level paradoxes, including the question of when and how salvation occurs, how the properties of the Trinity make salvation possible, and the paradox of whose choice determines our eternal salvation or eternal separation and how it does so. We have but scratched the surface. Much more work remains to be done.

When we who accept the authority of Christ and His Word encounter doctrinal disparity on a particular issue, such as spiritual gifts and the necessity of baptism, we can be assured of the need to delve into the deeper questions and paradoxes on which our conflict rests and work toward resolution at these deeper levels.[28] If we will use our disagreements as opportunities to grow in oneness through doing research and seeking greater depths of wisdom and understanding, we may find more nonbelievers attracted to our faith and interested in our dialogue, or at least in our preference for dialogue over debate.

The following chapters address the paradoxical nature of some sensitive issues—evil and suffering, the new creation, and the place Scripture calls the "lake of fire." Our struggles with such subjects only indicate that we have much room to learn and grow, and much need to ask help of the Holy Spirit, our Counselor and Guide.

CHAPTER FIFTEEN

EXTRA-DIMENSIONALITY AND EVIL AND SUFFERING

If a nonChristian were to ask us about any of the controversial topics addressed in preceding chapters, we probably would be ready
to converse. Many, if not most of us, would be thrilled at the chance
to discuss our beliefs on these subjects and the basis for them. Yet
there is one issue—the one we are about to explore—that seems
to tie our tongues more than any other, even among ourselves. And
this is the issue most frequently raised by atheists and other skeptics. They view it as our Achilles heel; no other reason has been
more widely offered for rejecting the God of the Bible. That subject
is evil and suffering.

Einstein was neither the first nor the last to discover that the
"problem of evil and suffering" is typically treated by Christians
and adherents to other religions as an unanswerable problem, a
mystery we can never in this life understand or explain.

Few have been so bold as C. S. Lewis in delivering public lectures
on it. Some books and essays have been written about it, but in general, our silence is deafening. Reasons for this silence abound. Experience tells us that the person asking why a loving, all-powerful God
would allow evil and suffering may have faced some horrific tragedy.
Our hesitancy to respond comes from recognition that a glib answer
will only intensify their anguish and confusion. The person asking
may also be seeking an argument or an occasion to embarrass us.
Given the emotional charge attached to this issue, no wonder it
proves daunting, even to the most learned students of Scripture.

A reply affirming that a good answer exists may be the most

helpful response when the question comes up, especially when the occasion does not permit a lengthy discussion. At least this reply opens the door for future dialogue and expresses the conviction that God did shed some light on this subject. His Word does address it from many angles, including head on, and we are able to see this if we step back a bit from the text to take a wide-angle look at God's message. Where does it start? Where does it end?

The challenge we can take up ourselves and pass along to inquirers calls for a reading (or rereading) of the first few chapters of the Bible and the last few. This review of "initial conditions" and "final conditions" can give us a fresh perspective on what unfolds in between and can help us discover some good and necessary purposes for the evil and suffering God allows in this world. Not that such a view offers a comprehensive response to such a difficult question. But it does provide us with an important context to consider a more complete answer.

First, one great irony must be exposed. Many who argue that the existence of evil and suffering proves the nonexistence of an all-powerful, all-loving Creator have no idea that it proves just the opposite. Naturalistic materialism, the notion that the natural world accounts for itself and needs no outside explanation, cannot account for the evil and cruelty we see among humans. Survival of the fittest does not result in the behavior humans exhibit all over the planet toward the land itself and toward animals and fellow humans.

Too Much Evil

Though the words sound shocking, we can reasonably say that the quantity of evil expressed on earth exceeds by far what atheistic evolutionary explanations can account for. Only the real existence of God and of His adversary, Satan, and the biblical account of God's purpose for this life, make sense of evil and suffering.

In case the ensuing discussion leads to assertions that "evolution" negates God and is solidly grounded in fact, we may want to be ready with a brief citation of some facts, which evolutionary biologists admit (some willingly, others reluctantly) contradict a non-theistic (that is, a materialistic) thesis (see table 15.1).

Table 15.1: Some Scientific Evidences Contradicting a Non-Theistic Interpretation of Speciation and Life's Origin
These evidences are taken from my previous books, *The Creator and the Cosmos*[1] and *Creation and Time*,[2] plus a short article.[3] Citations of the scientific literature are included therein.

1. Severe limits have been established on what changes and rates of change are possible via natural selection and mutations.
2. Natural selection leads much more often to stasis than to divergence.
3. Some species' populations are limited much less by starvation and predation than by instinctively controlled breeding or other behavior.
4. Only species with extremely large populations and short generation times can change significantly through mutations and natural selection. Only a few such species exist.
5. Speciation of animals since the appearance of humans (when God ceased creating) has dropped to a virtual zero by contrast with the abundant speciation before that time.
6. For the vast majority of animal species, change in the chemical makeup of the genes is so slow that, if it does occur, it cannot be observed.
7. While the fossil record indicates that certain genes must have changed very rapidly, chemical experiments document the impossibility of such rapid changes occurring under natural conditions.
8. Chemical differences within specific modern species are too small and between species too great for such species to be descended from a common ancestor by natural processes.
9. Regardless of their theological or philosophical preferences, most researchers admit that the universe's maximum age, even if it were twenty billion years, is insufficient by countless orders of magnitude to account for life's origin by any strictly natural explanation.
10. The geophysical record establishes that life arose on Earth in a time span briefer than ten million years under chemical conditions impossible for the assembly of life molecules by natural processes.
11. In a five-million-year window about 540 million years ago, a hundred new phyla appeared. No new phyla have appeared since. In fact, only thirty remain.

But sometimes a more effective approach may be to stick with our assertion that biological processes alone cannot be the source of the behavior patterns we see among humans. If survival of the fittest were the dominant force shaping humanity, we might see some chaos and randomness, but not the kind of evil and suffering that fills our headlines daily.

We humans are different from all other species. Both anthropology and theology attest to our uniqueness as spiritual creatures.[4] Our spirit component gives us a powerful capacity both for expressing goodness and for expressing evil. Unlike other species, we can inflict suffering on others for a variety of motives from revenge to perverse pleasure. Unlike other species, we kill for sport, and we tend to kill the best—the trophy animals—rather than the sick and weak. As for killing our own species, Leninist and Stalinist Russia, Nazi Germany, Maoist China, revolutionary France, Inquisitionist Spain and countless other modern societies (as well as ancient civilizations) show that we willingly slaughter and torture others.

How much of the injury and death and even disease-promoting behavior perpetrated by humans does anything to enhance the survival or well-being of the perpetrator? A reality check quickly informs us that we cannot chalk up the evil and suffering in our world simply to natural processes and survival instincts. Rather than proving the nonexistence of a spiritual realm and of a Creator-God, evil and suffering—even by our recognition of their repugnance—provide evidence for a good God opposed by some supernatural enemy, a God who for good reasons, some revealed in Scripture, is currently restraining the exercise of His almighty wrath against evil.

Return to Eden

How often we hear God's critics boast, "If I were in charge, I could have designed the world in such a way as to eliminate evil and suffering." Whether they admit it or not, such individuals see themselves as wiser and more righteous than God. If we are daring enough to ask for an explanation of what this human-designed, perfect world would be like, we may receive no answer. Or, most likely (in my experience, at least), we will hear a description that closely resembles Eden: a beautiful and pleasant paradise in which we would be protected from all harm for all time. Evil, if it did arise, would be snuffed out immediately so as not to afflict anyone but its source.

The Garden of Eden indeed was a wonderful place. Given the parameters of the universe, including its space-time boundaries and its laws of physics, no better environment for the human race could be constructed. Consider what Genesis says of our original parents' original environment:[5]

✦ The garden, designed and planted by the wisest and most loving of all beings, was perfectly beautiful, perfectly watered and fertilized, and perfectly free of weeds and pests.
✦ The plants of the garden pleased not only the eye but also the palate.
✦ The garden was full of treasures of all kinds, including gold, aromatic resin, and onyx.
✦ Adam and Eve had access to perfect health and unlimited longevity.
✦ Adam and Eve were given the capacity and the freedom to enjoy all the riches that abounded around them.
✦ They lived in perfect peace, harmony, and fellowship with all the animals.
✦ Adam and Eve enjoyed perfect peace, harmony, and fellowship with one another.
✦ They both enjoyed perfect peace, harmony, and fellowship with God.
✦ There was a complete absence of shame.

The biblical description of Eden reveals a human habitat unexcelled in human comprehension, at least not within our current reality's limits. Eden represents the best environment possible for the human race within the space-time continuum of the cosmos. We long for Eden because we long for the best our dimensional experience can suggest to our imagination. But God is not limited. His scope of operation exceeds by far our imaginative capacity. His plans for blessing humanity match His capacity to give—not our current, limited capacity to receive.

How many of us would rather return to Eden, to something good we can visualize, than to move beyond it to the new creation, which God says is better and yet which none of us can visualize? Atheists and agnostics are not the only ones who would rather stick with the familiar realm. Believers and unbelievers alike share this tendency. Many religious systems portray heaven as an Eden-like paradise often embellished with humans' sexual fantasies.

Analogy of the Exodus

An important depiction of the human tendency to prefer the familiar may be seen in the biblical account of the Hebrews' exodus from Egypt. Throughout the books of Exodus and Numbers we read of repeated confrontations between Moses and the masses. Again and again, because the promised land did not become immediately and easily accessible to them, the people begged Moses to forget about the promised land and lead them back to Egypt. There they had all the fish, cucumbers, melons, leeks, onions, and garlic they wanted.[6]

The ancient Hebrews' willingness to trade their freedom and a homeland flowing with milk, honey, fruit, grain, and mineral riches for hard bondage and a few vegetables and fish seems utterly unfathomable. From their perspective, however, the promised land remained unfathomable, mere words. Having never seen it for themselves and having no personal experience of freedom and prosperity, they lacked a vision and hope for what God had promised them. Though they acknowledged that the freedom and the promised land must be better than slavery in Egypt, they had difficulty recognizing that the difference was great enough to be worth a few months or years of hardship and suffering in the wilderness. Just as importantly, they failed to appreciate that without adequate preparation and training, which their hardship and suffering would provide, their ability to retain the blessings of the promised land would be short-lived.

We may be tempted to judge these people harshly, but we dare not, for we are so much like them. Our own experience and considerable psychological research reports that in nearly all circumstances, both children and adults will choose something good that is familiar over something better but unfamiliar.

The children of Israel, similar to our own children and ourselves, could not seem to understand that their resistance to God's training program, as difficult as it may have been, only brought them far more difficulty. Their wilderness experience was scheduled to last fourteen and a half months.[7] But their rebellion cost them forty extra years of desert wandering.[8]

Nearly one-fifth of the Bible is devoted to the exodus story. One reason I see for God's giving it so much space is that it reflects the ongoing journey of the entire human race. As the Hebrews set out from Egypt—a land of onions, garlic, and slavery—the human race set out from Eden—a paradise where humans were slaves to the threat of rebellion and sin. Though Adam and Eve were at first free from sin, they were also free-will beings with the capacity to receive and express love, which meant they or their descendants could choose to rebel against God's authority and reject His goodness. As many Hebrews died in unbelief and rebellion in the wilderness, so too, much of humanity will die without believing or embracing the eternal destiny God has promised. Those Hebrews who did follow God into the land were blessed with seeing the glory of God and receiving the bounty of that place. So, too, those who follow Christ into the new creation will be blessed with seeing His glory face-to-face and with receiving the bountiful rewards of that unimaginable place.

God had the option to lead the Hebrews from Egypt to Canaan along the north coastal road.[9] By that route the journey would have lasted only five to ten days. No one would have suffered. Much less evil would have been expressed and experienced. But, if God had chosen this option, the Hebrews would have been inadequately prepared to handle the many challenges, both physical and spiritual, of conquering and maintaining the new territory.[9] To avoid new forms of evil and suffering, they could have returned to the familiar hardships of Egypt. But the strength they gained from their new trials and troubles prepared them to seize and keep the land of their dreams.

The analogy here with the human race is that God could take away our current evil and suffering. But if He did, we might lose the capacity to gain and keep access to the new creation. At best, we think we could return to Eden, but not in the same condition as when we left. The Hebrews, too, deceived themselves in thinking they could return to Egypt as it was before the unleashing of the ten plagues.

We might be tempted to wish that God would take us to the new creation with a little less evil and suffering than we must face in this life. Again, the Hebrews' journey through the wilderness suggests why He does not fulfill that wish. In spite of the forty-one years of "training" they underwent, and even with the help of all the miracles God showed them both in Egypt and in the promised land, they were barely able to gain possession of the land. Eventually they lost their grip on it and only regained it, partially, in recent years. The history of Israel indicates that God did not overtrain these people.

Likewise, we can be assured that God is not overtraining us. We know how much motivating the Hebrews needed to undertake the exodus out of Egypt. They experienced much evil and suffering and many supernatural proofs of His power and protection. And we know how much motivating we need of a similar nature to undertake the exodus from sin's captivity. Still more evil and suffering, along with miraculous reassurances, moved the Hebrews along toward possession of the promised land. We, too, need more evil and suffering, along with God's miraculous reassurances, to move us along through the process of sanctification so that we will be ready for the splendors of the new creation.

Not all the evil and suffering we endure comes for our benefit alone. Sometimes God allows us to experience evil and suffering so that others may benefit also. Stephen, who was stoned to death by an angry mob of religious leaders, seems to exemplify this point. Holding the coats for that crowd, and seeing the radiant faith and face of the "villain" was a young zealot named Saul, whom God later transformed into the apostle Paul.[10]

If we want to shorten the span of this training program we find ourselves in, we can do it. Just as the Hebrews could have shortened their wanderings by cooperating with God and following Moses' instructions, we can cooperate with God more fully than we have by bending every effort and investing more resources toward completion of Christ's assignment to us. That assignment, which we call the Great Commission, could be carried out in our lifetime. Our struggles with evil and suffering will end when we successfully, by His enabling, bring the gospel and raise up disciples in every ethnic group on earth. That goal is within reach of the physical and spiritual resources of Christians, and it has been for some time, as determined by researchers at the United States Center for World Missions. While remarkable progress has been made within the last fifteen years,[11-12] we need increased faith and wider involvement among His people to make way for His coming.

Forward to the New Creation

A great boost toward that end and a greater sense of purpose in enduring evil and suffering will be ours when we turn our focus away from the paradise lost and toward the new creation to be gained. This theme resounds throughout the Bible.[13] Paul states it succinctly in his letter to believers at Philippi:

> Forgetting what is behind and straining toward what is ahead, I press on toward the goal to win the prize for which God has called me heavenward in Christ Jesus.[14]

Because the new creation is extra-dimensional and thus impossible to visualize, pressing toward it seems difficult to maintain at times. I have observed during my years in the classroom on both sides of the lectern that students who look forward to years of exciting research and discovery in physics or astronomy consider a few semesters of "torment" a small price to pay for the thrills that lie ahead. Those who have greatest difficulty in handling the "torment" and for whom the semesters drag have no great anticipation for such thrills. They are just preparing to support themselves and perhaps a family.

To have a clear vision of the reward ahead can be helpful, but we need more than that to spur us onward. Unless we place a high personal value on the reward, we will resent or perhaps seek escape from the pain and evil involved in reaching it. To latch onto the Christian faith because someone else thinks the new creation makes a superb travel destination will not get us through the tough times. We must want to go there for our own personal reasons. The author of Hebrews points to Jesus' life as a prime example of anticipation's impact:

> Let us fix our eyes on Jesus, the author and perfecter of
> our faith, who for the joy set before him endured the cross,
> scorning its shame, and sat down at the right hand of the
> throne of God. Consider him who endured such opposi-
> tion from sinful men, so that you will not grow weary and
> lose heart.[15]

We cannot see as clearly and directly as Jesus did the joy that awaited Him at the end of His sufferings, but neither are we called upon to suffer as He did. We may endure hardship and persecution at the hands of evildoers, but the people I have met who have suffered most intensely, including Russian and Chinese believers imprisoned for years and tortured horribly, also express emphatically that these sufferings, as awful as they were, "are not worth comparing with the glory that will be revealed in us."[16] These individuals, even without a perfect view of the reward awaiting them, had enough tangible evidence of its reality and a sufficient taste of its quality, to place a high personal value on it. Therefore, they endured.

We can all do more to enhance our capacity for endurance and enthusiasm for the difficulty of life's training program.[17] Though we cannot in four-dimensional thinking visually picture the physical characteristics of the heavenly realm beyond our earthly existence, we can exercise our spiritual capacity, our eyes of faith, to examine all the clues given in Scripture and develop a composite of its spiritual characteristics. Such an exercise can only (and richly!) increase our hope and anticipation for what soon awaits us.

> Dear friends, now we are children of God, and what we
> will be has not yet been made known. But we know that
> when he appears, we shall be like him, for we shall see him
> as he is. Everyone who has this hope in him purifies him-
> self, just as he is pure.[18]

But before we consider what we can now know of the new creation, we have one more hurdle to clear: What can we say in response to the question of a loving God who would consign individuals to the torments of hell?

CHAPTER SIXTEEN

GOD'S EXTRA-DIMENSIONAL LOVE IN HELL

Comprehending how God can express His love and care through our experience of evil and suffering may be difficult, but that conundrum remains orders of magnitude below the struggle—many would say the impossibility—in comprehending how that love is reflected in the Christian doctrine of hell.

Time and space, and physical and spiritual boundaries apply to evil and suffering. God promises that we will never face temptation beyond what we can bear, that He will always provide a "way of escape." But hell offers no escape. God also tells us the Holy Spirit acts as a restraining influence in the world right now, holding back the expression of evil. But hell offers none of the dimensional, physical, or spiritual boundaries we know. For God even to tolerate, let alone create, a place such as hell and to consign multitudes of His creatures to it, seems unthinkable, a contradiction of His biblically claimed attributes of omnipotence and perfect love.

The doctrine of hell, or "the lake of fire,"[1] as a place of perpetual torment for those who reject God's offer of salvation has been part of Christian orthodoxy for centuries.[2] Recently, however, especially in the last few decades, the perceived failure of theologians to reconcile eternal torment with an infinitely loving God has led to erosion of that doctrine.

To a large degree, this erosion has resulted from the tendency of late twentieth-century theology to view God's dealings with humanity in more and more human-like terms. An example comes from this excerpt of a published statement from the Seventh-Day

Adventist denomination:

> The most serious problem is that [the doctrine of hell] turns
> God into a monster. Hitler, at least, was merciful enough to
> put his victims out of their misery. But God, we are told,
> will artificially sustain human beings, keeping them alive
> just so they can suffer throughout eternity—and all this to
> pay for the misdeeds of a few short years on this earth.[3]

The statement continues to explain why hell cannot be located
anywhere in the universe but here on earth and, further, why its
location on earth, our "future paradise," must be short-lived indeed.
The exegetical flaws in this doctrinal statement, including its identification of heaven as an earthly paradise, can be refuted without
much difficulty.

The argument for the monstrous cruelty of a God who would
torment people eternally, however, is harder to sweep aside. In fact,
this argument recently persuaded the Church of England to change
its doctrinal position. After ten years of study, the church's doctrinal committee declared in 1996 that "a fiery eternal hell speaks of a
cruel sadistic God" and, since the Bible clearly teaches that God is
neither cruel nor sadistic, a correct interpretation of the Bible would
lead to the conclusion that "if a person refuses God's offer of salvation, the consequence is ultimate non-being."[4]

Extra-Dimensionality of Hell

If the doctrine of hell is treated as anything other than a paradox,
such either-or conclusions are unavoidable. An all-powerful, all-
loving God who tortures people infinitely for finite crimes—a four-
dimensional, anthropomorphic contradiction—thus demands
"adjustment."

First, the Bible makes clear that the lake of fire exists beyond,
not within, the dimensions of the universe (just as the new creation
does). The lake of fire and the new creation both survive God's
"rolling up" the entire physical universe and replacing it with something entirely new, including new (to us) dimensions or realms and
new physical and spiritual characteristics.[5]

God's purposes in creating the universe include fulfillment of His plan to conquer evil once and for always.[6] When that plan is fully accomplished at the Great White Throne Judgment,[7] God then removes the whole physical universe from existence.[8] But the new creation and the lake of fire are not the only created entities that will remain beyond this dramatic end. Every human who has ever lived and every angelic being also survives.[9] Apparently, one of the spiritual laws describing God's reality is that every spirit creature, once created, exists forever.

Ultimate non-being describes the fate of the universe, not the fate of unrepentant human beings and fallen angels. In other words, the doctrine of annihilation has been misapplied. God's plan does not call for eradication of sin and sinners from the universe, but rather it calls for eradication of the universe while sinners (because they are spirit beings) will never be eradicated. Neither sin nor sinners are anywhere present in the new creation. Twice in the last two chapters of Revelation, John records that sinners will continue to exist in the lake of fire after the Great White Throne Judgment— but never inside, always outside, the new creation.[10]

When the universe's matter, energy, and space-time dimensions no longer exist, the new creation and the lake of fire do exist. This information indicates that hell occupies a different dimensional realm from the one familiar to us. This point may represent a coincidence, but it seems worth mentioning. The biblical references to heaven and hell as somewhere "up" or "down" is completely appropriate from an extra-dimensional standpoint. Just as the screen people's correct description of a third spatial dimension would be "up" or "down," so, too, for us three-dimensional humans the proper description for any extra space dimension(s) or realms would be "up" or "down." Thus, when certain Bible verses refer to heaven as "up" and hell as "down," they do not suggest that heaven is in the sky and that hell is in the earth's core, but rather that heaven and hell reside in some kind of extra-dimensional realms.

The biblical descriptions of hell also suggest its extra-dimensionality. Just as the biblical account of the new creation's rewards and blessings presses hard against the limits of human imagination (see chapter 17), so does the account of hell's agonies. In fact, they clearly go beyond anything we can fully comprehend, no matter how graphic the descriptions.

Any solution to the paradox of eternal torment and God's love that can be completely understood in our four space-time dimensions must be incorrect. A satisfactory resolution will require us to look beyond the context of our human experience of love and torment. Such experience provides an inadequate and inappropriate basis for rejecting the reality of hell—and for comprehending how it fits with God's love.

Eternal Rebellion

A temporary sentence to hell for sin might indeed be appropriate if the sinner were merely paying "for the misdeeds of a few short years on this earth." This line of reasoning minimizes the meaning of sin and ignores the eternality of human choice, given the eternality of the human spirit. An individual who knowingly refused to worship God during this earthly life will never change his or her mind. Heaven's price, worshiping God and God alone, this person will never willingly pay. This person does not want to be in God's presence and, thus, would find heaven repugnant. As Hebrews says, "no sacrifice for sins is left" for those who knowingly discard God's sacred gift.[11] They may regret their eternal plight but not their rebellion.

Jesus clearly taught that nobody dies without having a clear and adequately understood opportunity to receive or reject His offer of forgiveness from sin and of eternal life with Him.[12] No person alive has totally missed "hearing God's call."[13-14] Ignorance of God and His offer comes from distorting and defying the truth He gives each person and, thus, is self-imposed.[15]

Hell is a place people choose. While the people in hell will despise their torment, they have demonstrated their preference for it over eternal fellowship with God and with all who love the Light.[16] For them, the experience of such fellowship would be far less tolerable than the torment of hell.

The lake of fire is a place where people and demons get what they want more than anything else: freedom from the will and rule of God. He yields to the desires of committed rebels by withdrawing forever the influence of His Spirit from their beings.

Scriptures Attesting Eternal Torment

The book of Revelation is most explicit in declaring that hell is a place of ongoing agony for its inhabitants:

> There is no rest day or night for those who worship the beast and his image.[17]

> The two of them [the beast and the false prophet] were thrown alive into the fiery lake of burning sulfur.[18]

> And the devil, who deceived them [the nations], was thrown into the lake of burning sulfur, where the beast and the false prophet had been thrown. They will be tormented day and night for ever and ever.[19]

> If anyone's name was not found written in the book of life, he was thrown into the lake of fire.[20]

Some interpreters of Revelation seek to avoid the force of these passages by claiming that we cannot determine where Revelation is literal and where it is symbolic. Yet while Revelation does employ more symbols than do most other books of the Bible, its writer defined each symbol either in the immediate context or with reference to the portion of Scripture in which it has been previously employed and defined. In these particular passages, we do see metaphoric language—but only to underscore the message of enduring torment.

Each of the Gospels also records descriptions of hell. Jesus spoke of it many times in His teaching, sometimes in parables, but usually in direct communication. The following statements come from His lips:

> "He will clear his threshing floor, . . . burning up the chaff [unbelievers] with unquenchable fire."[21]

"It is better for you to enter life maimed or crippled than to have two hands or two feet and be thrown into eternal fire."[22]

"Then he will say to those on his left, 'Depart from me, you who are cursed, into the eternal fire prepared for the devil and his angels.'" [23]

·"It is better for you to enter the kingdom of God with one eye than to have two eyes and be thrown into hell, where 'their worm does not die, and the fire is not quenched.'"[24]

Jesus' quotation of Isaiah's words affirm the metaphoric picture the prophet draws of the contrasts between hell and the new creation.

Jude in his epistle made reference to what happened to the people of Sodom and Gomorrah as an example, or warning, of "the punishment of eternal fire."[25] The Bible contains many more verses affirming that hell is real, enduring, and painful. And yet far more of Scripture is devoted to declaring and illustrating God's loving, merciful character. To be consistent with biblical revelation, any resolution of the paradox of God's love and hell's torment must uphold the truth of God's love, hell's existence, and hell's everlasting torment.

God's Compassion Expressed in Hell

These words may sound strange, but in light of God's character and the character of those sentenced to hell, those who inhabit the lake of fire occupy the best possible realm for them. God expresses His love and compassion for hell's inhabitants by afflicting them with sufficient torment to prevent the place from being as bad as its inhabitants have the capacity to make it.

We can only begin to imagine what evil could be expressed by those from whom the restraining influence of God the Spirit has departed. The unleashing of individuals' full potential for cruelty and all manner of evil could make hell vastly more horrible than God designed it to be. The worst thing about hell might be the company its inhabitants must keep. But God will keep in check the horrors these individuals could inflict on one another by immobilizing them, distracting them sufficiently with some kind of pain or discomfort.

The measure of pain and discomfort necessary to restrain each individual in hell will be different. Revelation speaks of differing levels or degrees of torment for those who are sent to hell, torment that is commensurate with each individual's earthly expressions of sin and rebellion.[26] The measure of wickedness a person practiced on earth is the measure of that individual's potential to make life more miserable than it already must be for others in hell. One interpretation suggests that God calibrates each person's torment to exactly the level necessary for restraint of his or her potential for evil.

A story might help to illustrate. If the public statements and writings of Adolf Hitler and Albert Schweitzer are indicative of where each of them finished their lives spiritually, then both could be described appropriately as rebels against God's authority. Again, if their public lives offer any reliable indication, Hitler expressed more wickedness than Schweitzer. Since both appear to have rejected God's truth and His offer of life in heaven's kingdom, we would assume both will spend eternity in hell. But because Hitler would seem to possess the greater capacity to multiply suffering, we can imagine that he would require more torment to keep his capacity for evil at bay.

The necessity of torment makes us aware that sin is far more grievous than any human can imagine. Because God's Spirit blunts the impact of sin in our world, we tend to underestimate its horror and in the process minimize what Christ took on Himself at the cross. If we have ever had dealings with an individual anywhere near blasphemy's threshold, the chill of that encounter should help us more accurately grasp what Christ suffered and what dangers hell's torment prevents.

None of this is meant to imply that the restraint of evil and suffering through torment is all that hell is about. My discussion here is not intended to be a full exposition of the doctrine of hell but simply to demonstrate that hell's torment is compatible with God's love.

Is *Torment* the Right Word?

The statements by the Church of England and the Seventh-Day Adventist Church expose what may be, at least partially, a semantic problem. Many who reject the reality of hell do so because they equate the word *torment* with "sadistic cruelty." The concept of a necessarily painful restraining effect seems to have been overlooked.

While the Greek word for torment in the early New Testament manuscripts can denote torture, it is also used for "grievous pains" or "distress."[27] New Testament writers used the same word to refer to the pains of childbirth.

Because the torment of hell is an extra-dimensional phenomenon, Bible writers faced serious limits in their attempt to communicate it. God's love, too, is an extra-dimensional phenomenon impossible to communicate fully in words. But we humans, even with our limited understanding, can find contexts in which a measured infliction of pain and an expression of love can be consistent. At that point we have taken a significant step toward demonstrating that God's use of some kind of pain and discomfort as a restraint in hell does not necessarily contradict His loving nature and consistent expression of love. And if an example of consistency can be found in our finite realm, surely greater possibility for consistency exists in God's extra-dimensional realm.

An illustration of the benefit of torment is one used in the preceding chapter: A professor "torments" his students for a semester to help prepare them for future success. A better analogy is that of a mother who inflicts her child with the "torment" of a car seat to protect him or her as they ride. Civilized societies incarcerate criminals to keep their citizens from further harm at the hands of lawbreakers.

A good friend of mine once stumbled into a real-life lesson on the consistency of God's love and His restraint of evil-doers in hell. Through the simple error of misreading a map, he was arrested for selling film on the wrong side of the street in the vicinity of Pasadena's Rose Bowl.

Under normal circumstances he would have been driven to the courthouse, cautioned by a judge, and released. But because so many revelers had been arrested the night before, the court system was jammed. All the Pasadena jail cells were full, as were those in the neighboring communities. My friend, who had never even been sent to the principal's office during his school years, was sent to Los Angeles County Jail not just for a few hours but for a whole day and night.

He was placed in a cell with eight other men. While the Los Angeles police do their best to separate the violent felons from the rest of the inmate population, their efforts are limited. My friend glanced around to meet eight pairs of eyes staring at this obvious first-timer, each more fearsome than any he had encountered in his life, including his travels to foreign lands. Eight men watched, waiting for him to fall asleep. He spent that day and night awake and praying, his back glued to the cell wall.

No physical harm came to him during those agonizing hours, but he does remember wishing that an officer would come to handcuff and leg cuff the others so that he could get a moment's rest. Those cuffs would have brought torment, of course, but certainly no more than the torment my friend endured. From his perspective, the most loving thing the police could have done was to restrain his cell mates with cuffs. But what if some of them didn't really need the cuffs? The most loving scenario for the total group would have been for the police to provide the greatest restraint to the most dangerous inmates, lesser restraint for those less dangerous, and no restraint for those who would do no harm to the others. Unfortunately, neither the police nor anyone else can see that clearly into people's hearts. But God can. And since God does see, He would know precisely how dangerous each of hell's inhabitants can be. With this knowledge, He would be able to determine precisely what degree of restraint to apply to each individual. And that could be considered an act of love.

How much better, though, to experience His love where it can be fully and freely expressed, in the place He is preparing for our eternal fellowship with Him and with one another—the place for which He is preparing us.

CHAPTER SEVENTEEN

EXTRA-DIMENSIONALITY AND THE NEW CREATION

If hell stretches beyond the limits of our imagination, so does heaven. Many, if not most, people who say they want to go there can point to only one reason: They know they want to be with. . . . Believers typically fill in the blank with "Jesus," or "God," or perhaps "God and all His children." Nonbelievers usually fill in the name of their favorite deceased loved one or friend. Rarely in my life have I heard anyone express much more than this one anticipation of the place. Sometimes people's desire to go there reflects more honestly their wish to avoid hell, in case such a place exists.

Because of children's honesty, they are usually the ones to admit their worry that heaven might be boring, a place where we will all resemble the angels (as depicted in Renaissance paintings), ride around on clouds, and play harps or sing praise songs all day (which means all the time since night does not exist in heaven). I cannot help but wonder how many adults harbor this same concern. Seldom do we in our churches and fellowships talk about heaven. Christ's thousand-year reign on earth—for those who accept the doctrine of the Millennium—seems to generate more discussion. And that makes sense because it seems to resemble the Garden of Eden in some ways. But the biblical descriptions of the new creation sound so strange to us, so far beyond familiar experience—streets paved with gold as clear as glass, for example—that we tend to abandon all earthly images and, thus, all discussion.

Yet the heavenly "prize" is supposed to represent the motivation for pressing on through the tribulations of this life. Apparently we need to dig a little more deeply into Scripture to gain a clearer view and deeper appreciation for whatever awaits us in the new creation. Because of what we know about God and about the absence of evil there, we can be sure the new creation is better than anything in this earthly life. In that case, a game of "Heaven is better than . . ." can be especially helpful to children, and beneficial for believers of all ages.

Extra-Dimensionality of the New Creation

Two statements at the beginning of Revelation 21 affirm that the new creation exists in dimensions (or their equivalent) entirely independent of the ones we now experience:

> I saw a new heaven and a new earth, for the first heaven and the first earth had passed away.[1]

> The old order of things has passed away. He who was seated on the throne said, "I am making everything new!"[2]

God's brand-new creation will be completely different, according to these verses, from our familiar universe. This proclamation that the old order of things will pass away and that everything will be made new suggests that no physical entities will be carried over from the old creation into the new creation. "Physical" will have a new meaning. All the forces and laws of physics will be changed.

This brand-newness seems consistent with God's pattern of creative work. Just as God's first creation "week" begins with God's "speaking into existence" something entirely new—a universe of matter, energy, and dimensions for their distribution and operation (see chapter 5, pages 41-43)—so, too, God begins His second creation by introducing a brand new realm, a new "heaven and earth," denoting the dwelling place of God and of humans. The new "earth" will have entirely new properties.

Electromagnetism and gravity operate on material objects in three dimensions of space. Stable atom structure and stable planetary and star orbits, for example, are impossible in anything other than three dimensions of space. Evidence that gravity will be different or nonexistent in the new creation comes from the biblical description of the New Jerusalem. The new "city of peace" rests on the new earth and is laid out as a cube, 12,000 stadia (1,379 miles or 2,219 kilometers) long, 12,000 stadia wide, and 12,000 stadia high.[3] If the familiar force of gravity were in operation, this cube would collapse into a spherical shape, for in our universe, any material object with dimensions exceeding about 300 miles across would be pulled by gravity into a more or less spherical shape.

We cannot assume, however, that the new creation will be devoid of any kind of physicality. If the place were nonphysical in every way, the use of "measuring rods" would make no sense.[4] It is hard to conceive, too, of nonphysical gates, streets, walls, and mountains.[5] More significantly, when Jesus appeared to His disciples after the resurrection, He affirmed both verbally and tangibly that His resurrection body had certain physical, though obviously different, characteristics and capacities.[6] Other Scriptures indicate that we who go with Christ into the new creation will receive new bodies, very different from our present ones, but bodies nonetheless.[7]

Further evidence for different physical laws comes from statements about the absence of decay processes in the new creation. Paul tells us that the law of decay is temporary, limited to the present cosmos:

> Our present sufferings are not worth comparing with the glory that will be revealed in us. The creation waits in eager expectation for the sons of God to be revealed. For the creation was subjected to frustration, not by its own choice, but by the will of the one who subjected it, in hope that the creation itself will be liberated from its bondage to decay and brought into the glorious freedom of the children of God.[8]

The apostle John records that death, mourning, crying, and pain will no longer be part of the new creation.[9] Apparently, we will consume without incurring any cost, further indication of decay's absence.[10] If decay is not in effect there, neither is the second law of thermodynamics. That law states the existence of processes bringing increasing disorder or decay, necessary to the operation of the cosmos we know but obviously having no part in the new one. And yet, the texts on the new creation indicate that God, the angels, and we humans will all possess the capacity to perform what could technically be defined as "work." The possibility of work without the second law of thermodynamics in effect means that a dimensionality totally different from ours must exist there.

The most convincing evidence for the extra-dimensionality of the new creation comes from the biblical descriptions of our relationships with God and with one another — also from descriptions of our enjoyment of the place.

New Creation Travelogue

While John did see some aspects of the new creation, most of what he passes on to us is what one of God's angels told him about its features. Paul may have been given a glimpse of the new creation,[11] but he was told to keep silent about what he saw. Isaiah offers a description at the close of his prophetic book, while Ezekiel, Joel, and other prophets make several brief mentions in their books. Jesus in His earthly ministry gave us the most thrilling information about life in His future kingdom.

All these descriptions suggest the enormity of our new habitation. If its population exceeds ten billion, the New Jerusalem alone would give each of us about forty billion cubic feet of living space (equivalent to a fourteen square mile home with a hundred foot high ceiling). What we will do exactly with all that space we cannot yet know. However, our habitat will be better than all the splendors of this earth, from its ocean depths to its mountain grandeur.

Whatever structures Jesus may have meant when He spoke about the "mansions,"[12] they must be magnificent indeed, considering His eye for beauty as seen even in this limited world. Furthermore, no forces in the new creation will cause the wearing down of what He makes — or what we may make, given the extension of our capacities for creativity. Imagine what our lives would be like if the time and energy we now expend on maintenance and upkeep could be devoted wholly to creative pursuits!

Not only is the new creation free of deterioration, but it is also free of natural and manmade disasters and crime, all the things that so seriously drain our wealth in this world. In our familiar world, wealth of all kinds, material and relational, must be protected, and the costs of such protection increase with the value of what needs protecting. In the new creation, our wealth will not burden us. God can and will bless each of us with an inheritance beyond what we can possibly dream. The Bible says that in the new creation we will inherit everything that Christ inherits.[13]

The New Jerusalem represents just one portion of our new domain. And since the New Jerusalem's size exceeds earth's largest structures by more than ten trillion times, the new earth's proportions probably supersede the present earth's by a similar factor. Though the New Jerusalem will be roomy enough to serve as "home" for every believer, we will have full access to the new earth, and the new heavens will also be available for our enjoyment.

The increase in our mobility will be dramatic. What makes *Star Trek* and other space travel movies and television shows difficult for physicists to enjoy is their pervasive violations of physical laws. We do not know of any ways to transport people to distant stars and galaxies without overriding the laws of physics or the physical limitations of our bodies. Even visiting the planets in our solar system may be beyond our reach. We have been unable to find a practical means to protect humans in space, long term, from meteorites, solar radiation, and cosmic radiation. Such limitations, including the law of gravity, will no longer hamper our travel in the new heavens and the new earth.

Safe from Harm

The absence of pain in the new creation implies that the risks of injury and illness will be gone. Though in Eden pain was reduced, it was still present,[14] for Adam and Eve did not possess indestructible bodies and thus needed some pain sensation to warn them of injury or of impending injury. We who choose life in the new creation will all receive indestructible bodies.[15] Our bodies will experience no injury, no sickness, no pain, no weakness.

Hunger and thirst will also be things of the past.[16] No longer will our bodies need food, rest, exercise, repair, or other maintenance. Never again will our bodies let us down. Never again will we have to say, "The spirit is willing but the flesh is weak." Experiencing no more hunger, thirst, and weakness refers to much more than physical matters. We will be completely and continuously "full" and satisfied — physically, emotionally, intellectually, and spiritually. While our lives today bring us moments of satisfaction, the perfect and sustained satisfaction for which we yearn will finally be ours to possess forever in the new creation.

Revelation tells us that sorrow and crying will be past experiences. Their absence suggests that grief and regret will also be past. We will have no cause for grief in the new creation, for we will never experience loss or injustice or tragedy of any kind. Fellowship will never be broken. Nothing of value to us will ever be diminished. As we recall the former creation, we will have the necessary understanding to recognize that everyone did fulfill the potential for which he or she was created. Those we knew and loved who chose the lake of fire over the new creation will have been treated with utmost fairness and goodness.

The characteristic of the new creation most frequently emphasized in the biblical passages is the absence of darkness.[17] The light of God's glory illuminates everything, and everything radiates or reflects God's light. Just as the sun casts no shadow, nothing in the new creation casts shadows. Darkness, even shades of darkness, cannot be found. Again, the Bible speaks of this light without shadows not just in a physical sense but in an emotional, intellectual, and spiritual sense as well.

Relational Wonders

As dramatic as the alterations in our environment may seem, the relational changes will be more profound. In the new creation no one will fear, hide, or deceive. No one will experience envy or doubt. No one will demean or in any way violate the sanctity of another creature, and no one will exalt anything or anyone above God.[18] Every barrier that prevents or limits intimacy between us will be removed for all eternity. Instead, everyone in the new creation will consistently exhibit the character and love of Jesus Christ in all circumstances and for all time.[19]

There will be no boors or bores in the new creation. Never again will any of us experience the slightest cringing when we see an individual moving toward us. Because we will be healed of all brokenness and distortions, each individual in the new creation will be someone we delight to commune with, much more than we do now with our favorite person on Earth.

Each of us in the new creation will be given an assignment for which we are perfectly suited. We will have some kind of roles to fulfill as "rulers" over the angels and over whatever God creates in the new kingdom.[20] We will work together in perfect peace and harmony for all of eternity. All of us in the new creation will be one as God is one.[21] We will be in one accord with God and with one another, and yet each of us will retain some distinct identity and the freedom to choose. Through the training we are now experiencing, we will become adequately convinced of the benefits of choosing what is good and true and will be empowered to make those good and true choices (see chapters 13 and 14).

Intimacy Without Sexuality

Jesus explicitly stated during His earthly ministry that in the new creation there would be no nuclear families, no marriage as we now experience it, and no sexuality.[22] Many nonChristians, when they hear these truths about heaven, begin to wonder if Christianity is worthwhile. "How can heaven be paradise without sex?" they wonder.

A preliminary answer is that God never takes away anything from us without replacing it with something better. Such an answer, while it is true, typically falls on deaf ears unless we can go on to describe what that "something better" could possibly be. The problem here is that many people can think of no pleasure superior to sex. Outside of Judaism and Christianity, most religions and cults distort and abuse the sexuality God gave us either in their teachings about the afterlife or in their teachings about earthly relationships and worship practices. Their teachings are either overly restrictive or overly indulgent. In some ironic cases, they are severely restrictive in this earthly life and promise extreme indulgence in the afterlife. These writings reflect the human tendency, perhaps more prevalent among males, to exalt the pleasures of sex above all else. Thus, in its unique perspective on sexuality both in earthly relationships and in heavenly ones, the Bible reflects the inspiration of a transcendent Being.

While much of human thinking and teaching emphasizes the physical side of sex, the Bible focuses on its spiritual and relational aspects. According to the Bible, what heightens the enjoyment of sex and the exploration of its pleasures is not the use of certain physical techniques but the degree of oneness a man and woman have developed in the broad spectrum of their relationship—in their spiritual, emotional, intellectual, and relational values, for example. To build this oneness, a man and a woman must invest generously in their relationship. Because of our current limits in this four-dimensional universe, achieving maximum intimacy requires us to concentrate our resources on one individual to the exclusion of others.

This exclusion principle has application beyond the marriage relationship. Again, because of our space-time context, even our capacity to build friendships is limited. We can choose to have a few close friends and a few dozen casual friends. But time, energy, and other resource limits prevent us from building an unlimited number of close friendships.

We face the frustration of such limits continually in this life. Wherever we go, whatever we do, we meet people whose personalities we enjoy and with whom we would like to become better acquainted, possibly building a close and enriching relationship. We see this potential, and yet we must choose to follow through with only a select few if we wish to maintain our balance and responsibilities. In this sense, one thing that made Eden a paradise was its population: two.

Intimacy's New Depth and Breadth

The biblical pictures of the new creation suggest the absence of virtually all relationship-limiting factors. Christ often refers to believers in the new creation with singular nouns and pronouns.[23] Specifically, Jesus refers collectively to believers in the new creation as His bride, and He says that we all will be one as He, the Father, and the Holy Spirit are one. The oneness of all believers refers to

God's presence with all of us simultaneously and to our unity in love and truth. Such oneness dramatically enhances our relationships with each other. But, there may be more.

The oneness of the Godhead would be impossible unless the Father, Son, and Spirit are in continuous communication and fellowship with one another. For us to experience the same kind of oneness we, too, would need to be in continuous communication and fellowship with one another. We might gain the capacity to communicate and relate intimately with billions of others all at once—and agree perfectly with each one.

Our present dimensionality makes such simultaneous communication and fellowship impossible. But with one extra dimension of time or its equivalent, we could acquire this capacity. As God can listen and respond to any number of prayers simutaneously in two time dimensions (see chapter 7, pages 64-65), so we may be able to give our full attention to countless other believers simultaneously—and receive theirs.

That is not to say we will become omnipresent. Just as our current ability to make conference calls to several individuals on different continents does not imply we are everywhere on Earth at once, so, too, our possible capacity for simultaneous communion with many billion individuals would not imply that we are present everywhere in the new creation.

With this new capacity for knowing and being known by, loving and being loved by all other human beings in the new creation, our need for marriage and a nuclear family is fully met. We no longer will need to focus our relationship resources on one spouse, our own children, our other family members, and our selected friends. We will continuously enjoy with all other members of the heavenly family something far superior to the pleasures of the very best of times in our earthly relationships, including marriage.

We will all personally commune with those individuals of all ages whom we have admired most and longed to know. Think of the crowds surrounding Jesus as He traveled and taught on earth. People had to wait their turn to see Him and talk to Him, and many who were less patient than Anna and Simeon,[24] less persistent than Zacchaeus,[25] and less resourceful than the men who lowered their friend through a roof[26] never did get that privilege. In the new creation such difficulties and disappointments will vanish. We will all be able to fellowship with God and with one another as we please, and with greater intimacy than any of our earthly relationships yet allow.

The people who most fear the loss of sexual relationships in the new creation are most likely those who abuse such relationships. When people feel the pain of disconnection in one or more key relationships, they may tend to ease that pain with sex rather than deal with the pain and brokenness. They hope a sexual union will restore or perhaps replace the love bond they lack. As alcoholics use alcohol to dull the pains and sorrows in their lives, so do many use sexual encounters. But, in the new creation, the love and understanding we need will be fully available to us. The gnawing pain caused by love deficits will be healed, and no anesthetics for that pain will be sought.

Marriage will not be missed because our earthly marriages will be replaced by one unimaginably superior marriage. All believers in the new creation will experience such relational pleasure and one accord with each other and with God that we will all relate as one bride to one groom.

We who are married now will be married in the new creation, not just to our current marriage partner, but to Christ as well. Right now we are engaged to Christ,[27] and our engagement gives us the potential to experience a wonderful, growing personal relationship with Him. That relationship takes nothing away from our earthly marriages. In fact, it enhances them. When we become the bride of Christ, the joy and fulfillment of our relationship with Him will be multiplied far beyond the best it can be now. Yet that multiplication will take nothing away from the relationships we have with our earthly marriage partners—nor will it detract from any other relationship.

The new creation is a place where none of us will ever need to say goodbye to anyone. We will all be together forever. But our desire for privacy will be taken care of as well. Given that we may possess something like the equivalent of two time dimensions, we would have a near infinite number of time lines for maintaining relationships. After we subtract ten billion or so to accommodate all the people in the new creation, another hundred million plus for the angels,[28] billions more for whatever new creatures God may create, we will still have a near infinite number of time lines for solitary reflection, projects, hobbies, and pastimes if we want them.

While our human capacity will be vastly expanded in the new creation, we will not become God or gods. We will never become omnipresent, omniscient, or omnipotent. We will never gain the ability to create something from nothing. Nor will we necessarily gain power advantage over angels. Our role as judges over them has more to do with direction and authority than with power.

Multiplication of God's Glory and Love

We human beings were created to give glory to God and to reflect His love. Our participation in God's plan to conquer evil totally and permanently fits into these purposes. This is true, too, for developing a Christlike character. In the new creation we will be liberated and empowered to glorify God many times beyond what we can conceive of now. Having been delivered permanently from sin, evil, and suffering, we will be free to love as we have never loved before. With the new capacities with which God will endow us, we finally will know through direct experience just how magnificent His love is. We also will have the capacity to *receive* love from God and others many times beyond what we can conceive of now and to *give* love to God and others many times beyond what we can conceive of now.

Our ability to receive honor and love from God to an unimaginable degree and to express this honor and love to others will enable us to join Christ in managing much of the new creation and in participating with God in the fulfillment of His plans beyond those we know.

All that has been revealed to us in Scripture concerning God's future plans extends just into His eighth day of creation. We know only the beginning of the future. If the beginning is so staggeringly magnificent, then the remainder of eternity with Him will surely hold blessings that stretch still farther beyond our ability to imagine. We can only stand in awe and anticipation of something we comprehend as good, and there find a purifying, perpetually motivating hope. Full satisfaction, happiness, and peace await us in our heavenly home.

CHAPTER EIGHTEEN

AN INVITATION
TO SOAR HIGHER STILL

Extra dimensions are simply new terms to describe truths that have been known for as long as God has been known by any human. The beauty and benefit of these terms and the recent scientific discoveries undergirding them lies both in their affirmation of what Scripture has always proclaimed about God's transcendence and in their potential to help us explore and make sense of the Bible's transcendent teachings that are being challenged more intensely than ever by the "rationalists" of our time.

This integration of science and theology will be welcomed by some and resisted or repudiated by others. It may be misconstrued by those who think any scientific application to biblical texts and doctrines compels us to walk by sight rather than by faith. Actually, the opposite is the case. Many of our traditional approaches to discovering theological truths have suffered from the limitations of a four-dimensional, or "sight," perspective. Extra dimensions cannot be seen, cannot reflect our human perspective, because they exist beyond the present cosmos. Scientists have found them not by seeing them but by discovering their importance for the universe's existence. In other words, they have unwittingly rediscovered the necessity of a God whose characteristics just happen to match the capacities needed to explain our existence.

The apostle Paul grasped extra-dimensionality long ago, as did the prophet Isaiah, whom he quotes in these words to the Corinthian church:

"No eye has seen, no ear has heard, no mind has conceived what God has prepared for those who love him"—but God has revealed it to us by his Spirit. The Spirit searches all things, even the deep things of God. For who among men knows the thoughts of a man except the man's spirit within him? In the same way no one knows the thoughts of God except the Spirit of God. We have not received the spirit of the world but the Spirit who is from God, that we may understand what God has freely given us.[1]

Paul's inspired message expresses the apologetics theme of this book. These verses speak of eternal salvation and blessing, not just the future heaven, which God has prepared for us who love Him. Our eyes cannot picture it, our ears cannot catch it on physical sound waves, our four-dimensional thinking could never have given birth to it—and yet God's Spirit has opened our hearts to receive it.

The faith to "see" God both in and beyond the extra dimensions from which our universe began comes not from ourselves, as Paul says, but from the Spirit of God. It is the Spirit who alone can reveal to us an extra-dimensional God and enable us to understand the extra-dimensional salvation offered by the Father, transacted by the Son, and imparted by the Holy Spirit.

The amazing discoveries in particle physics and astrophysics highlighted in the opening chapters of this book take none of the mystery away from "the deep things of God." If anything, they distinguish for the skeptics of our day the mysteriousness of divine truth from the imaginativeness of human fantasy. The discoveries indicating the existence of extra dimensions simply attest that God's power and wisdom and all other capacities exceed ours by so many orders of magnitude that they bear no resemblance to human, four-dimensional thinking.

✦ What other God but the God revealed in the Bible promises to be nearer to each of us than we are to ourselves, beyond the reach of our physical senses, yet fully within the reach of the spiritual sense He placed within us?

✦ What other God but the God revealed in the Bible claims
to have planned and initiated the physical universe from
dimensions beyond and independent of it?

✦ What other God but the God revealed in the Bible can
see and hear everything, including the thoughts and
prayers of every living being at every moment?

✦ What other God but the God revealed in the Bible has
come tangibly to affirm His existence, His power, His
truth, and His love through a human body, seeking no
glory for self in that body but for God alone?

✦ What other God but the God revealed in the Bible claims
to be simultaneously singular and plural—Father, Son,
and Holy Spirit, not three gods but a triune deity—and
proves His capacity to be such?

✦ What other God but the God revealed in Christ's body
could take upon Himself the penalty for humanity's
waywardness and could wield the power to rise bodily
from the dead?

✦ What other God but the God revealed in the Bible could
accurately communicate through human authors the
distinctive capacities of His created life forms, from
plants to animals to mammals and birds to humans, in
terms that scientific research thousands of years later
proves precisely accurate? And what mind could con-
trive such creatures as He calls angels, archangels,
cherubim, and seraphim?

✦ What other God but the God revealed in the Bible shows
total character consistency in all His messages to and
dealings with the human race?

✦ What other God but the God revealed in the Bible finds
a way to give humans freedom of choice and yet works
within that freedom to fulfill all His divine purposes and
plans?

✦ What other God but the God revealed in the Bible could
devise a way to secure our eternal destiny while retain-
ing forever our freedom to choose or reject Him?

✦ What other God but the God revealed in the Bible could

design and administer a pass or fail "heart" test for each
human being with the exact degree of difficulty and
time allowance appropriate for his or her ability to
respond? Who but God could make full use of that test
as preparation for our future career in His new creation?

✦ What other God but the God revealed in the Bible could
find a way to express love toward those beings who hate
Him and choose eternal separation from His authority
and glory?

✦ What other God but the God revealed in the Bible
promises His children an inheritance remotely like the
new creation; a place that makes Eden look paltry and
pale by comparison; a place where we will find the perfection of love, joy, and wholeness for which we all have
perpetually yearned?

✦ What other God but the God revealed in the Bible
would provide for us, as Boaz provided for Ruth, not
just the gleanings from the harvest of scientific truth, but
"six measures of barley"—geometrically multiplying
evidences of His intention to provide for all our faith
needs in this increasingly irreverent, arrogant, self-
destructing world?

The connections made in this book between scientific data
(specifically about extra dimensions) and scientific methods (specifically the application of paradox resolution steps to traditionally
divisive biblical doctrines) represent not a fixed set of conclusions
and solutions, but a suggestion of where to begin a new chapter in
our age-old pursuit of spiritual truth and understanding. God
knows that our intellectual and technological advances have raised
new questions and doubts about our ultimate origin, ultimate destination, and thus our ultimate purpose and responsibility. The pace,
complexity, and instability of modern life has crowded and clouded
our thinking so that we need extra help in "holding onto that which
is good," holding onto childlike trust in Him and His Word.

God invites us to make good use of the new discoveries about
extra dimensions (among other aspects of His creative work) for

building that trust and for breaking through barriers that hamper our relationships with Him, with each other, and with those outside the faith. We can run away from these findings and maintain our current course, or we can embrace them and find fresh vitality in our study and exposition of Scripture. The current course seems a path of growing rigidity and damaging division. The push to separate issues of fact from issues of faith is strong and gaining momentum among those who seem to fear truth more than love it. But the potential for healing and reconciliation, revitalized faith and zeal for outreach lies in this new direction, which God has opened to us.

These discoveries about extra-dimensionality bear the potential to boost significantly Christians' awareness of the extent of power God has made available to us. As Jesus declared, if we know the resources God has made available to us, we can accomplish great things, the great things He has planned all along for us to do.[2] Imagine what would happen in this world if we Christians were to vastly enlarge our vision of God's capacity to empower us, to protect us, to use us in fulfilling His plans and purposes, and to reward us!

Such a vision would change us. Our appreciation for His Word would change. Our thought life would change. Our prayer and worship would change. Our relationships would change. Our effectiveness in reaching the world's unbelievers would change. The results would be dramatic on all fronts. Perhaps this is part of how Christ's prayer will be answered: "May they be brought to complete unity to let the world know that you sent me and have loved them even as you have loved me."[3]

The end of this book is really a beginning point. God will continue to give us His Light to understand truth as we continue to pursue understanding together, as we live and serve together as children of the Light. We can rejoice even now that He is preparing us for life in the full Light of His glory (sunglasses no longer needed).

NOTES

Chapter One: An Invitation to Soar

1. 2 Timothy 2:13, *The Holy Bible: New International Version* (NIV).
2. Mark 9:24, NIV.

Chapter Two: Takeoff from Ground Zero

1. Silk, Joseph, *The Big Bang*, revised and updated edition (New York: W. H. Freeman, 1989), pp. 90-96, 165.

Chapter Three: Science Breaks Through to New Realms

1. Ross, Hugh, *The Fingerprint of God*, second edition (Orange, Calif.: Promise, 1991), pp. 42-49.
2. Ross, Hugh, *The Creator and the Cosmos*, second edition (Colorado Springs, Colo.: NavPress, 1995), pp. 19-47.
3. Ross, Hugh, "News Report Hypes Cosmic Age Controversy," *Facts & Faith*, vol. 8, no. 4 (1994), pp. 1-2.
4. Ross, Hugh, "Hubble Constant Conflict Update," *Facts & Faith*, vol. 9, no. 1 (1995), pp. 3-4.
5. Mather, J. C., et al., "Measurement of the Cosmic Microwave Background Spectrum by the COBE FIRAS Instrument," *Astrophysical Journal* 420 (1994), pp. 439-444.
6. Hancock, S., et al., "Direct Observation of Structure in the Cosmic Background Radiation," *Nature* 367 (1994), pp. 333-338.
7. Clapp, A. C., et al., "Measurements of Anistropy in the Cosmic Microwave Background Radiation at Degree Angular Scales Near the Stars Sigma Herculis and Iota Draconis," *Astrophysical Journal Letters* 433 (1994), pp. L57-L60.
8. Songaila, Antoinette, et al., "Measurement of the Microwave Background Temperature at Redshift 1.776," *Nature* 371 (1994), pp. 43-45.
9. Meyer, David M., "A Distant Space Thermometer," *Nature* 371 (1994), p. 13.
10. Douglas, A. Vibert, "Forty Minutes with Einstein," *Journal of the Royal Astronomical Society of Canada* 50 (1956), p. 100.
11. Barnett, Lincoln, *The Universe and Dr. Einstein* (New York: William Sloane Associates, 1948), p. 106.

12. Eddington, Arthur S., "The End of the World: From the Standpoint of Mathematical Physics," *Nature* 127 (1931), p. 450.

13. Eddington, Arthur S., "On the Instability of Einstein's Spherical World," *Monthly Notices of the Royal Astronomical Society* 90 (1930), p. 672.

14. Bondi, Herman, *Cosmology*, second edition (Cambridge, UK: Cambridge University Press, 1960), p. 140.

15. Hoyle, Fred, "A New Model for the Expanding Universe," *Monthly Notices of the Royal Astronomical Society* 108 (1948), p. 372.

16. Hoyle, Fred, *The Nature of the Universe*, second edition (Oxford, UK: Basil Blackwell, 1952), p. 109.

17. Hoyle, *The Nature of the Universe*, p. 111.

18. Dicke, R. H., Peebles, P. J. E., Roll, P. G., and Wilkinson, D. T., "Cosmic Black-Body Radiation," *Astrophysical Journal Letters* 142 (1965), p. 415.

19. Tolman, Richard C., and Ward, Morgan, "On the Behavior of Non-Static Models of the Universe When the Cosmological Term Is Omitted," *Physical Review* 39 (1932), p. 842.

20. Barrow, John D., and Silk, Joseph, *The Left Hand of Creation* (New York: Basic, 1983), p. 32.

21. Penrose, Roger, "An Analysis of the Structure of Space-Time," *Adam Prize Essay*, Cambridge University (1966).

22. Hawking, Stephen W., "Singularities and the Geometry of Space-Time," *Adam Prize Essay*, Cambridge University (1966).

23. Hawking, Stephen W., and Ellis, George F. R., "The Cosmic Black-Body Radiation and the Existence of Singularities in Our Universe," *Astrophysical Journal* 152 (1968), pp. 25-36.

24. Hawking, Stephen, and Penrose, Roger, "The Singularities of Gravitational Collapse and Cosmology," *Proceedings of the Royal Society of London*, series A, 314 (1970), pp. 529-548.

25. Weinberg, Steven, *Gravitation and Cosmology: Principles and Applications of the General Theory of Relativity* (New York: J. Wiley and Sons, 1972), p. 198.

26. Shapiro, Irwin I., et al., "Mercury's Perihelion Advance Determination by Radar," *Physical Review Letters* 28 (1972), pp. 1394-1397.

27. Pound, R. V., and Snider, J. L., "Effect of Gravity on Nuclear Resonance," *Physical Review Letters* 13 (1964), pp. 539-540.

28. Brans, C., and Dicke, R. H., "Mach's Principle and a Relativistic Theory of Gravitation," *Physical Review* 124 (1961), pp. 925-935.

29. Vessot, R. F. C., et al., "Test of Relativistic Gravitation with a Space-Borne Hydrogen Maser," *Physical Review Letters* 45 (1980), pp. 2081-2084.

30. Moffat, J. W., "Consequences of a New Experimental Determination of the Quadrupole Moment of the Sun for Gravitation Theory," *Physical Review Letters* 50 (1983), pp. 709-712.

31. Taylor, J. H., et al., "Experimental Constraints on Strong-Field Relativistic Gravity," *Nature* 355 (1992), pp. 132-136.

32. Penrose, Roger, *Shadows of the Mind* (New York: Oxford University Press, 1994), pp. 229-231.

33. Penrose, p. 230.

34. van der Meer, Simon, "Stochastic Damping of Betatron Oscillations in the ISR," *CERN/ISR-PO/72-31* (1972), pp. 1-8.
35. Arnison, G., et al., "Experimental Observation of Isolated Large Traverse Energy Electrons with Associated Missing Energy at $\sqrt{s}$ = 540 GeV," *Physics Letters* 122B (1983), pp. 103-116.
36. Banner, M., et al., "Observation of Single Isolated Electrons of High Transverse Momentum in Events with Missing Transverse Energy at the CERN pp Collider," *Physics Letters* 122B (1983), pp. 476-485.
37. Arnison, G., et al., "Experimental Observation of Lepton Pairs of Invariant Mass Around 95 GeV/$_c$2 at the CERN SPS Collider," *Physics Letters* 126B (1983), pp. 398-410.
38. Abe, F., et al., "Evidence for Top Quark Production in pp Collisions at $\sqrt{2}$ = 1.8 TeV," *Physical Review* D, 50 (1994), pp. 2966-3026.
39. Abe, F., et al., "Identification of Top Quarks Using Kinematic Variables," *Physical Review* D, 52 (1995), pp. R2605-R2609.
40. Cole, K. C., "Two Physicists Simplify Study of Four-Dimensional Space," *Los Angeles Times*, 29 November 1994, pp. A1, A29.
41. Taubes, Gary, "How Black Holes May Get String Theory Out of a Bind," *Science* 268 (1995), p. 1699.
42. Taubes, Gary, "A Theory of Everything Takes Shape," *Science* 269 (1995), p. 1513.
43. Peterson, Ivars, "Beyond the Top: Now that Physicists Have Found the Top Quark, What's Next?" *Science News* 148 (1995), pp. 10-12.
44. Lamoreaux, S. K., et al., "New Limits on Spatial Anistropy from Optically Pumped 201Hg and 199Hg," *Physical Review Letters* 57 (1986), pp. 3125-3128.
45. Ross, Hugh, *The Creator and the Cosmos*, second edition (Colorado Springs, Colo.: NavPress, 1995), pp. 112-121.

Chapter Four: Science's Tethers

1. Davies, Paul, *God and the New Physics* (New York: Simon & Schuster, 1983), pp. vii-8. In Paul Davies' newest and most exhaustive treatment of this subject, *The Mind of God* (New York: Simon & Schuster, 1992), he alters his original position to the belief that the complete mind of God is possibly, not probably, within man's grasp (pp. 14-15).
2. Hawking, Stephen W., *A Brief History of Time* (New York: Bantam, 1988), pp. 155-175.
3. Tipler, Frank J., *The Physics of Immortality* (New York: Doubleday, 1994), pp. 2-10.
4. Ross, Hugh, *The Fingerprint of God*, second edition (Orange, Calif.: Promise, 1991), pp. 41-43.
5. Silk, Joseph, *The Big Bang*, revised and updated edition (New York: W. H. Freeman, 1989), pp. 90-96, 165.
6. Harrison, Edward, *Masks of the Universe* (New York: Collier, 1985), pp. 178-184.
7. Eisberg, Robert M., *Fundamentals of Modern Physics* (New York: John Wiley & Sons, 1961), pp. 153-162.
8. Messiah, Albert, *Quantum Mechanics*, vol. I (New York: John Wiley & Sons, 1966), pp. 129-149, 299-301.

9. Eisberg, pp. 146-162, 468-472, 662-664, 695-703.

10. Silk, pp. 119-124.

11. Ferris, Timothy, "Science and Genesis," *Cosmic Beginnings and Human Ends* (Chicago, Ill: Open Court, 1995), pp. 38-39.

12. Kolb, Edward W., "The Big Bang Origin of the Universe," *Cosmic Beginnings and Human Ends* (Chicago, Ill: Open Court, 1995), pp. 72-74.

13. Psalm 19:1-4.

14. Deuteronomy 29:29, *The Holy Bible: New International Version*.

Chapter Five: Extra Dimensions in the Bible

1. Harris, R. Laird, Archer, Gleason L., and Waltke, Bruce K., *Theological Wordbook of the Old Testament*, vol. I and II (Chicago: Moody Press, 1980), pp. 74-75, 935.

2. Waltke, Bruce, *Creation and Chaos: An Exegetical and Theological Study of Biblical Cosmogony* (Portland, Ore.: Western Conservative Baptist Seminary, 1974), pp. 20, 25-26.

3. Harris, Archer, and Waltke, p. 127.

4. Hebrews 11:3, *The Holy Bible: New International Version* (NIV).

5. 2 Timothy 1:9, NIV.

6. Titus 1:2, NIV.

7. Proverbs 8:22-23, NIV.

8. John 17:5,24, NIV.

9. Ephesians 1:4, NIV.

10. 1 Peter 1:20, NIV.

11. Harris, R. Laird, Archer, Gleason L., and Waltke, Bruce K., *Theological Wordbook of the Old Testament*, vol. I (Chicago: Moody Press, 1980), pp. 74-84.

12. Brown, Colin, ed., *The New International Dictionary of New Testament Theology*, vol. I (Grand Rapids, Mich.: Zondervan Publishing House, 1975), p. 524.

13. John 1:3, NIV.

14. Colossians 1:16-17, NIV.

15. Nave, Orville J., *Nave's Topical Bible* (Chicago, Ill.: Moody Press, 1974), pp. 434-438.

16. Psalm 90:4, NIV.

17. Martyr, Justin, "Dialogue With Trypho, chapter 81," Writings of Saint Justin Martyr, in *The Fathers of the Church*, vol. 6, Ludwig Schopp, editorial director (New York: Christian Heritage, 1948), pp. 277-278; Irenaeus, "Against Heresies," book V, chapter XXIII, section 2, *The Ante-Nicene Fathers*, vol. I, ed. Alexander Roberts and James Donaldson (Grand Rapids, Mich.: Eerdmans, 1981), pp. 551-552; Lactantius, "The Divine Institutes, Book VII, Chapter XIV," in *The Ante-Nicene Fathers*, vol. VII, p. 211; Victorinus of Pettau, "The Created World, Book VI," in *The Ante-Nicene Fathers*, vol. VII, p. 342; Methodius of Olympus, "Fragment," in *The Ante-Nicene Fathers*, vol. VI, p. 310.

18. 2 Peter 3:8, NIV.

19. John 20:9, Luke 24:37-43, NIV.

20. Luke 24:39-40, 1 John 1:1, NIV.

21. Luke 24:42-43, John 21:7-15, NIV.

22. Isaiah 37:21-38, NIV.

23. 2 Kings 2:1-18, NIV.
24. Acts 8:26-40, NIV.
25. Luke 9:28-36, NIV.
26. Isaiah 38:7-8, 39:1, NIV.
27. Ross, Hugh, *Fulfilled Prophecy: Evidence for the Reliability of the Bible* (Pasadena, Calif.: Reasons To Believe, 1978).
28. Philippians 2:5-11, NIV.

Chapter Six: Extra-Dimensional Doctrines

1. Packer, J. I., *Knowing God* (Downers Grove, Ill.: InterVarsity Press, 1993), pp. 222-223.
2. Geisler, Norman, and Howe, Thomas, *When Critics Ask: A Popular Handbook on Bible Difficulties* (Wheaton, Ill.: Victor, 1992).
3. Archer, Gleason L., *Encyclopedia of Bible Difficulties* (Grand Rapids, Mich.: Regency Reference Library, 1982).
4. John 7–9, *The Holy Bible: New International Version*.
5. Packer, pp. 222-223.
6. Ross, Hugh, *The Fingerprint of God*, second edition (Orange, Calif.: Promise, 1991), p. 42.

Chapter Seven: God and Extra Time Dimensions

1. Psalm 139:17-18, *The Holy Bible: New International Version*.
2. Plato, Parmenides, 140d-141e; Timaeus, 36e-39e, *The Collected Dialogues of Plato*, ed. Edith Hamilton and Huntington Cairns (New York: Pantheon Books, Bollingen Series LXXI, 1961), pp. 934-935, 1166-1168.
3. Augustinus, Aurelius, and Bishop of Hippo, *Saint Augustine, The City of God*, books VIII–XVI, trans. Gerald G. Walsh and Grace Monahan (New York: Fathers of the Church, Inc., 1952), book XI, chapters 5 and 6, pp. 193-196.
4. Aquinas, Thomas, *Summa Theologica*, vol. 2 (New York: McGraw-Hill, 1964), Prima Pars 2, Existence and Nature of God, Question 10, The Eternity of God, pp. 135-155.

Chapter Eight: Extra-Dimensionality and God's Proximity

1. Genesis 16:13, *The Holy Bible: New International Version* (NIV).
2. Genesis 28:16, NIV.
3. 1 Chronicles 28:9, NIV.
4. 2 Chronicles 6:30, NIV.
5. Job 23:10, NIV.
6. Job 24:23, NIV.
7. Job 31:4, NIV.
8. Job 34:21-23,25, NIV.
9. Psalm 33:13-15, NIV.
10. Psalm 34:18, NIV.
11. Psalm 44:21, NIV.
12. Psalm 94:11, NIV.
13. Psalm 119:151,168, NIV.
14. Psalm 139:1-4,7-10, NIV.

15. Psalm 145:18, NIV.
16. Proverbs 5:21, NIV.
17. Jeremiah 23:24, NIV.
18. Jeremiah 32:19, NIV.
19. Matthew 10:30-31, NIV.
20. Matthew 28:20, NIV.
21. Acts 17:27, NIV.
22. Hebrews 13:5, NIV.
23. John 4:24, NIV.
24. Genesis 28:16, NIV.
25. Exodus 33:20, NIV.
26. Job 9:11, NIV.
27. Job 23:8-9, NIV.
28. Job 37:23, NIV.
29. Isaiah 45:15, NIV.
30. 1 Timothy 1:17, NIV.
31. 1 Timothy 6:16, NIV.
32. John 1:18, NIV.
33. John 5:37, NIV.
34. John 6:46, NIV.
35. John 13:33, NIV.
36. John 13:36, NIV.
37. John 13:37, NIV.
38. Since the payment for Peter's sins against God and others had not yet been paid and Jesus had not yet been raised from the dead, the Holy Spirit could not yet permanently indwell Peter. Peter himself explains this in 1 Peter 3:21.
39. John 14:2-3, NIV.
40. John 16:6-7, NIV.
41. John 16:20-22, NIV.
42. John 20:19, 21:1-22; Acts 1:6-12, NIV.
43. The Hebrew words for faith in the Old Testament are *emuna* and *emet*, whereas the Greek word used for faith in the New Testament is *pistis*. *Emuna*, *emet*, and *pistis* all basically mean acting upon what one has established to be true and trustworthy [Packer, J. I., "Faith," in *Evangelical Dictionary of Theology*, Walter A. Elwell, ed. (Grand Rapids, Mich.: Baker Book House, 1984), pp. 399-401; Harris, R. Laird, Archer, Gleason L., and Waltke, Bruce K., *Theological Wordbook of the Old Testament* (Chicago, Ill.: Moody Press, 1980), pp. 52-53; Vine, W. E., *Expository Dictionary of New Testament Words*, vol. II (Old Tappan, N.J.: Fleming Revell, 1940), p. 71].
44. 1 Chronicles 28:9, NIV.
45. James 4:8, NIV.
46. Psalm 145:18, NIV.
47. Psalm 34:18, NIV.
48. Isaiah 57:15, NIV.
49. Hebrews 11:6, NIV.
50. 1 Corinthians 15:50, NIV.
51. 1 Corinthians 15:52-53, NIV.

52. 1 Corinthians 15:42-44, NIV.
53. 1 John 3:2, NIV.

Chapter Nine: Extra-Dimensionality and God's Triunity
 1. Boice, James Montgomery, *The Sovereign God* (Downers Grove, Ill.: Inter-Varsity Press, 1979), p. 147.
 2. Genesis 1:26, *The Holy Bible: New International Version* (NIV).
 3. Genesis 1:27, NIV.
 4. Genesis 3:22-24, 11:7-8; Isaiah 6:8, NIV.
 5. Harris, R. Laird, Archer, Gleason L., and Waltke, Bruce K., *Theological Wordbook of the Old Testament* (Chicago: Moody Bible Institute, 1980), pp. 44-45.
 6. Manley, G. T., "Names of God," *The New Bible Dictionary*, ed. J. D. Douglas, et al. (Grand Rapids, Mich.: Eerdmans, 1962), p. 478.
 7. Isaiah 43:11-12, 45:21-22; Hosea 13:4, NIV.
 8. Isaiah 44:24, 45:18; Colossians 1:16-17; Revelation 4:9-11, NIV.
 9. Job 19:25; Isaiah 47:4, 49:6-7, 49:26, 54:5, 59:15-20, NIV.
10. Acts 1:22; 2:24,31; 4:33; 17:31-32; Romans 1:4; 6:5; Philippians 3:10; 1 Peter 1:3; 3:21, NIV.
11. Isaiah 63:16, Romans 8:11-15, 2 Thessalonians 2:13, 1 Timothy 1:1, 2 Timothy 1:10, Titus 1:4, NIV.
12. Genesis 1:2, Job 33:4, John 1:3, Colossians 1:13-17, James 1:17-18, NIV.
13. Matthew 28:6-7; John 2:19-21, 10:17-18; Acts 2:32; Romans 1:4, 6:4, 8:11; Galatians 1:1, NIV.
14. Jeremiah 23:5-6, NIV.
15. Matthew 28:19, NIV.
16. Boice, pp. 141-142.
17. Warfield, Benjamin B., "Trinity," *The International Standard Bible Encyclopaedia*, James Orr, ed. (Grand Rapids, Mich.: Eerdmans, 1983), pp. 3012-3013.
18. Grane, Leif, *The Augsburg Confession: A Commentary* (Minneapolis, Minn.: Augsburg Publishing House, 1987), pp. 31-32.
19. Macpherson, John, *The Westminster Confession of Faith* (Edinburgh, UK: T. & T. Clark, 1882), p. 44.
20. M'Crie, Charles Greig, *The Confessions of the Church of Scotland* (Edinburgh, UK: Macniven & Wallace, 1907), pp. 36-63.
21. Smith, Egbert Watson, *The Creed of Presbyterians*, revised and enlarged edition (Richmond, Va.: John Knox Press, 1941), p. 29.
22. Boice, pp. 142-145.
23. Boice, p. 141.
24. Ryrie, Charles C., *A Survey of Bible Doctrine*, study edition (Chicago: Moody Press, 1972), p. 33.
25. Bromiley, Geoffrey W., "Trinity," *Evangelical Dictionary of Theology*, ed. Walter A. Elwell (Grand Rapids, Mich.: Baker Book House, 1984), p. 1112.
26. Bromiley, pp. 1112-1113.
27. Finlayson, R. A., "Trinity," *The New Bible Dictionary*, second edition, ed. J. D. Douglas, et al. (Wheaton, Ill.: Tyndale House, 1982), pp. 1222-1223.
28. Finlayson, p. 1223.
29. Matthew 4:1-11, Luke 4:1-13, NIV.

30. Matthew 26:39,42,44, NIV.

31. Mark 14:33-34, Luke 22:44, NIV.

32. John 17:11,21-22, NIV.

33. John 17:23, NIV.

34. Ephesians 3:18-19, NIV.

Chapter Ten: Extra-Dimensionality, the Incarnation, and the Atonement

1. See Hebrews 2:14-18, 4:15.

2. Matthew 11:27, 12:28, 22:41-46, 28:18-20; Luke 10:22; John 5:17-23, 6:27, 8:58, 10:17-18,30-39, 14:6-11,16-26, 15:26, 16:7-15, 17:1-11,21-24, 20:27-29, *The Holy Bible: New International Version* (NIV).

3. Of the nine miracles John describes in any detail in his Gospel, all nine are miracles beyond what any prophet had ever performed and all nine were miracles that contemporary rabbis declared could be performed only by God Himself.

4. Hebrews 2:14, 4:15, NIV.

5. Matthew 1:18-25, NIV.

6. Luke 1:30-35, NIV.

7. Matthew 4:1-3, NIV.

8. Mark 4:39, NIV.

9. Hebrews 2:14, NIV.

10. Hebrews 2:17, NIV.

11. Hebrews 4:15, NIV.

12. John 8:46, NIV.

13. 1 John 3:5, NIV.

14. Romans 3:9-20, NIV.

15. Ephesians 2:8-9, NIV.

16. Luke 14:25-33, NIV.

17. John 3:16, NIV.

18. Romans 5:12-19, NIV.

19. Genesis 3:7-24, NIV.

20. Hebrews 1:3-14, NIV.

21. 2 Corinthians 5:21, NIV.

22. Matthew 12:39-40, NIV.

23. Coulter, Frederick R., *A Harmony of the Gospels in Modern English: The Life of Christ* (Los Angeles, Calif.: York, 1974), pp. 231-247.

24. John 16:8-11, NIV.

25. Romans 1:18-23, NIV.

26. Ecclesiastes 3:11, NIV.

27. Romans 8:29, 9:10-13, NIV.

28. Ephesians 1:4-14, NIV.

29. Romans 5:6, NIV.

30. Hebrews 2:9, NIV.

31. 1 John 2:1-2, NIV.

32. Mark 15:25,34-39, NIV.

33. Metherell, Alex, and Ross, Hugh, *Behold the Man*, video documentary (Pasadena, Calif.: Reasons To Believe, 1995).

34. Hebrews 9:11, NIV.
35. Hebrews 9:24-25,28, NIV.
36. Hebrews 9:11-18, NIV.
37. Hebrews 2:3, NIV.
38. Psalm 50:10, NIV.
39. John 20:24-29, 1 John 1:1, NIV.

Chapter Eleven: Dimensional Capacities of Created Beings

1. Revelation 12:4, *The Holy Bible: New International Version* (NIV).
2. Wieland, Carl, "Is Cruelty Normal?" *Creation Ex Nihilo*, vol. 16, no. 3 (1994), pp. 19-21.
3. Ham, Ken, "Adam and Ants," *Back to Genesis*, no. 33, September 1991, p. a.
4. Stambaugh, James S., "Death Before Sin?" *Impact*, no. 191, May 1989, p. ii.
5. Job 14:8-10, NIV.
6. Psalm 37:2, NIV.
7. Harris, R. Laird, Archer, Gleason L., and Waltke, Bruce K., *Theological Wordbook of the Old Testament* (Chicago: Moody Press, 1980), pp. 496-497.
8. Matthew 21:18-22, NIV.
9. Mark 4:35-41, NIV.
10. Exodus 7:18, NIV.
11. Exodus 7:21, NIV.
12. Exodus 8:13, NIV.
13. Proverbs 30:25, NIV.
14. Ecclesiastes 10:1, NIV.
15. Harris, Archer, and Waltke, pp. 587-591.
16. Harris, Archer, and Waltke, p. 701.
17. Harris, Archer, and Waltke, p. 127.
18. Brown, Colin, ed., *The New International Dictionary of New Testament Theology*, vol. III (Grand Rapids, Mich.: Zondervan Publishing House, 1978), p. 689.
19. Numbers 22:21-34, NIV.
20. Psalm 104:27-28, NIV.
21. Luke 14:5, NIV.
22. Matthew 10:29, NIV.
23. Harris, Archer, and Waltke, p. 10.
24. Penrose, Roger, *Shadows of the Mind* (New York: Oxford University Press, 1994).
25. Gazzaniga, Michael S., ed., *The Cognitive Neurosciences* (Cambridge, Mass.: The MIT Press, 1995).
26. Dennett, Daniel C., *Consciousness Explained* (Boston: Little, Brown and Company, 1991).
27. Hebrews 13:2, NIV. An example of communication where the form of the angel could not be perceived by the human participant is given in Job 4:12-17.
28. Genesis 18:1–19:29, Daniel 10:1-21, NIV.
29. Jeremiah 7:16, 14:10-12; 1 Corinthians 14:1-40; James 5:13-20; 1 John 5:14-17, NIV.
30. John 1:9, 3:19-21; Romans 1:18-21, NIV.
31. Ecclesiastes 3:11, NIV.

32. Romans 2:11-15, NIV.
33. Romans 3:9-20, NIV.
34. John 16:8-11, NIV.
35. Romans 12:1-2, Galatians 5:22-23, NIV.
36. 2 Corinthians 6:16, NIV.
37. Job 34:14-15, NIV.
38. Romans 12:9-21, 1 Corinthians 12:4-31, Ephesians 4:11-16, NIV.
39. John 10:10, NIV.
40. Matthew 17:20-21, NIV.
41. Matthew 21:21-22, NIV.
42. John 14:12-15, NIV.
43. John 15:7, NIV.
44. John 16:33, NIV.
45. 2 Corinthians 3:18, NIV.
46. 2 Corinthians 4:16-18, NIV.
47. Psalm 103:20, 2 Thessalonians 1:7, NIV.
48. Revelation 14:10, NIV.
49. 2 Peter 2:11, NIV.
50. Matthew 26:53, NIV.
51. 2 Kings 2:9-12, 6:15-18, NIV.
52. Daniel 10:4-8, NIV.
53. Isaiah 42:8, 43:10-11, 44:6, 45:5,22-24, NIV.
54. Revelation 7:2-3, 16:8-9, NIV.
55. Isaiah 44:24, Colossians 1:16-17, Revelation 4:11, NIV.
56. Matthew 22:30, NIV.
57. Genesis 6:2-4, Jude 6-8, NIV. A fuller exposition on this interpretation is given in my paper, *Sons of God . . . Who Are They?* (Pasadena, Calif.: Reasons To Believe, 1985).
58. Ephesians 3:10, 6:12; Colossians 1:16, 2:15, NIV.
59. Ezekiel 28:12-17, NIV.
60. Ezekiel 1, 10, NIV.
61. Revelation 4:6-8, NIV.
62. Harris, Archer, and Waltke, p. 884.
63. Isaiah 6:2-7, NIV.
64. Daniel 10:13, NIV.
65. Daniel 10:21, Jude 9, NIV.
66. Revelation 12:7-9, NIV.
67. Psalm 8:4-5, Hebrews 2:6-7, NIV.
68. Ephesians 1:8-10, 3:10; 1 Peter 1:12, NIV.
69. Daniel 7:18-27, 1 Corinthians 6:2-3, NIV.
70. Matthew 18:10, NIV.
71. Hebrews 1:14, NIV.

Chapter Twelve: God's Omnipotence Versus His Displayed Power

1. Numbers 23:19; 1 Samuel 15:29; Psalm 33:4, 100:5, 117:2, 146:6; Daniel 4:37; John 17:17; Titus 1:2; Hebrews 6:18, *The Holy Bible: New International Version* (NIV).

2. 2 Chronicles 19:7, Job 34:10, Psalm 5:4, Matthew 19:17, Luke 6:35, Romans 1:23, James 1:13, NIV.

3. Psalm 1:5, 5:4-5, 11:4-6; Habakkuk 1:13; Matthew 7:23, NIV.

4. Ecclesiastes 3:17, 11:9, 12:14, NIV.

5. Malachi 3:6, Romans 11:29, Hebrews 6:17-18, James 1:17, NIV.

6. Luke 18:18, NIV.

7. Luke 18:19, NIV.

8. 2 Peter 3:9, NIV.

9. 1 John 4:7-12, NIV.

Chapter Thirteen: Extra-Dimensionality and the Battle of Wills

1. Joshua 24:14-15, *The Holy Bible: New International Version* (NIV).

2. Joshua 24:19, NIV.

3. Joshua 24:20-27, NIV.

4. Exodus 33:19, NIV.

5. Acts 13:48, NIV.

6. Genesis 1:2, NIV.

7. 1 John 1:5–5:20, NIV.

8. Romans 8:1-17, 13:11; 2 Corinthians 10:4-5; Philippians 2:12-13; Colossians 1:28-29; 2 Thessalonians 3:3-5, NIV.

9. John 8:34-44, Acts 8:20-23, Romans 7:15-25, Colossians 2:8, 2 Timothy 2:22-26, NIV.

10. Romans 12:1-2, 2 Corinthians 4:14-18, Ephesians 4:22-24, Colossians 3:9-10, NIV.

11. John 8:34-44, Romans 1:18-32, 2 Thessalonians 2:9-12, NIV.

12. Revelation 22:13, NIV.

13. 1 Samuel 23:10-12; Isaiah 42:9, 46:9-11, 48:5-8; Daniel 2:28-29; Romans 8:29, 11:2; 1 Peter 1:2, NIV.

14. Exodus 3:13-14, John 8:58, NIV.

15. Romans 8:29, NIV.

16. Romans 9:11-13, NIV.

17. Romans 11:2,5, NIV.

18. 1 Peter 1:1-2, NIV.

19. Refer to Ross, Hugh, *Creation and Time* (Colorado Springs, Colo.: NavPress, 1994).

20. Job 38:22-30; Psalm 139:13-16; Proverbs 21:1; Ephesians 2:10, 5:15-17; Colossians 4:5-6; 1 Peter 3:13–4:19, NIV.

21. 1 Samuel 23:10-12, 1 Kings 22:19-22, Daniel 10:12–11:1, Acts 8:26-40, NIV.

22. 1 Corinthians 10:13, NIV.

23. Romans 8:28, NIV.

Chapter Fourteen: Extra-Dimensionality and Salvation's Security

1. 2 Corinthians 13:5, *The Holy Bible: New International Version* (NIV).

2. Psalm 33:11, 119:89; Ecclesiastes 3:14; Malachi 3:6; Romans 11:29; Hebrews 6:17-18; James 1:17, NIV.

3. Ross, Hugh, *The Fingerprint of God*, second edition (Orange, Calif.: Promise, 1991), pp. 179-183.

4. Galatians 5:22-23, NIV.

5. 2 Corinthians 1:21-22, 5:5; Ephesians 1:13-14; 2 Timothy 1:12, NIV.

6. Wuest, Kenneth S., *Wuest's Word Studies from the Greek New Testament*, vol. 2 (Grand Rapids, Mich.: Eerdmans, 1973), pp. 113-117.

7. Pink, Arthur W., *Eternal Security* (Grand Rapids, Mich.: Guardian Press, 1974), pp. 91-93.

8. 2 Peter 2:22, NIV.

9. Romans 8:38-39, NIV.

10. 2 Corinthians 1:21-22, 5:5; Ephesians 1:13-14, NIV.

11. Philippians 2:12, NIV.

12. 2 Peter 3:17, NIV.

13. 2 John 8, NIV.

14. Ephesians 2:8-9, NIV.

15. 1 John 5:16-17, NIV.

16. Exodus 7:13,22-23, 8:15,19,32, 9:7, *New American Standard Bible* (NASB).

17. Exodus 9:12,35, 10:20,27, 14:4, (NASB).

18. Mark 3:28-29, NIV.

19. Romans 1:24, NIV.

20. Romans 1:26, NIV.

21. Romans 1:28, NIV.

22. Ephesians 2:10, NIV.

23. Romans 12:1-2, NIV.

24. Ross, Hugh, *The Fingerprint of God*, second edition (Orange, Calif.: Promise, 1991), pp. 177-178.

25. Revelation 20:11-15, NIV.

26. Matthew 7:21-23, 23:1-36; John 8:19,23-26,37-47, NIV.

27. 2 Timothy 1:12, NIV.

28. Ross, Hugh, *Papers on Spiritual Gifts Packet* (Pasadena, Calif.: Reasons To Believe, 1987).

Chapter Fifteen: Extra-Dimensionality and Evil and Suffering

1. Ross, Hugh, *The Creator and the Cosmos*, second edtion (Colorado Springs, Colo.: NavPress, 1995), pp. 123-146.

2. Ross, Hugh, *Creation and Time* (Colorado Springs, Colo.: NavPress, 1994), pp. 48-50, 73-80.

3. Ross, Hugh, "Science in the News," *Facts & Faith*, vol. 9, no. 3 (Pasadena, Calif.: Reasons To Believe, 1995), pp. 1-5.

4. Ross, *Creation and Time*, pp. 140-141.

5. Genesis 2:8–3:24, *The Holy Bible: New International Version* (NIV).

6. Numbers 11:5, NIV.

7. Exodus 12:1-50; Numbers 9:1-5, 10:11-12, 13:1-30, NIV.

8. Deuteronomy 1:3-4, Joshua 4:19, NIV.

9. Exodus 13:17-18, NIV.

10. Acts 6:5–8:2, 9:1-22, NIV.

11. Winter, Ralph D., "The Diminishing Task," *Mission Frontiers*, vol. 13, no. 11-12 (1991), p. 36; "God's Symphony of Effort," *Mission Frontiers*, vol. 17, no. 3-4 (1995), p. 6.

12. Bush, Luis, "The Unfinished Task," *Mission Frontiers*, vol. 17, no. 3-4 (1995), pp. 7-14.

13. Deuteronomy 29:29; Isaiah 64–66; Ephesians 1:11-23, 3:7-20; Philippians 2:12-18, 3:12–4:1; Hebrews 12:1-2; Revelation 1–22, NIV.
14. Philippians 3:13-14, NIV.
15. Hebrews 12:2-3, NIV.
16. Romans 8:18, NIV.
17. James 1:2-4, NIV.
18. 1 John 3:2-3, NIV.

Chapter Sixteen: God's Extra-Dimensional Love in Hell

1. Revelation 19:20-21, 20:10,14-15, *The Holy Bible: New International Version* (NIV).
2. Lightner, R. P., "Hell," *Evangelical Dictionary of Theology*, ed. Walter A. Elwell (Grand Rapids, Mich.: Baker Book House, 1984), p. 506.
3. Moore, Marvin, "Where on Earth Is Hell?" *Signs of the Times*, January 1996, p. 29.
4. Announced on KFWB, 980 AM radio, Hollywood, California, shortly after 1:00 A.M., January 12, 1996.
5. Revelation 20:7–22:15, NIV.
6. Ross, Hugh, *Creation and Time* (Colorado Springs, Colo.: NavPress, 1994), pp. 65-69.
7. Revelation 20:11-15, NIV.
8. Revelation 21:1-4, NIV.
9. Ecclesiastes 3:11, Revelation 20:10–22:15, NIV.
10. Revelation 21:8, 22:15, NIV.
11. Hebrews 10:26, NIV.
12. John 3:15-21, NIV.
13. Ross, Hugh, *The Fingerprint of God*, second edition (Orange, Calif.: Promise, 1991), pp. 179-183.
14. Richardson, Don, and Ross, Hugh, *The Lord's Handiwork*, one-hour video documentary (Pasadena, Calif.: Reasons To Believe, 1991).
15. Romans 1:18-25, NIV.
16. 2 Timothy 3:1-9, 2 Peter 2, Jude 8-16, NIV.
17. Revelation 14:10-11, NIV.
18. Revelation 19:20, NIV.
19. Revelation 20:10, NIV.
20. Revelation 20:15, NIV.
21. Matthew 3:12, NIV.
22. Matthew 18:8, NIV.
23. Matthew 25:41, NIV.
24. Mark 9:47-48, NIV.
25. Jude 7, NIV.
26. Revelation 20:11-15, NIV.
27. Brown, Colin, ed., *The New International Dictionary of New Testament Theology*, vol. III (Grand Rapids, Mich.: Zondervan Publishing House, 1978), p. 856.

Chapter Seventeen: Extra-Dimensionality and the New Creation

1. Revelation 21:1, *The Holy Bible: New International Version* (NIV).
2. Revelation 21:4-5, NIV.

3. Revelation 21:16, NIV.

4. Revelation 21:15, NIV.

5. Revelation 21:10-21, NIV.

6. Luke 24:36-43, John 20:25-28, 1 John 1:1, NIV.

7. 1 Corinthinans 15:35-57, NIV.

8. Romans 8:18-21, NIV.

9. Revelation 21:4, NIV.

10. Revelation 21:6-7, NIV.

11. 2 Corinthians 12:1-6, NIV.

12. John 14:1-4, *King James Version*.

13. Romans 8:17, Ephesians 1:3, Revelation 3:21, NIV.

14. Ross, Hugh, *Creation and Time* (Colorado Springs, Colo.: NavPress, 1994), pp. 67-69.

15. Joel 2:2-11; 1 Corinthians 15:42-44,50-54, NIV.

16. Psalm 34:9-10, Isaiah 65:13, Revelation 7:16, NIV.

17. John 8:12; 2 Corinthians 4:6; 1 John 1:5; Revelation 21:23-25, 22:5, NIV.

18. Revelation 21:8, NIV.

19. 1 John 3:1-3, NIV.

20. Romans 8:17, 1 Corinthians 6:2-3, 1 Peter 2:9, Revelation 22:5, NIV.

21. John 17:11; Romans 12:5, 15:5-6; Revelation 21:9-27, NIV.

22. Matthew 22:29-32, Luke 20:34-39, NIV.

23. John 17:11; Romans 12:5, 15:5-6; Revelation 21:9-27, NIV.

24. Luke 2:25-38, NIV.

25. Luke 19:1-9, NIV.

26. Mark 2:1-12, NIV.

27. Ephesians 1:13-14, NIV.

28. Revelation 5:11, NIV.

Chapter Eighteen: An Invitation to Soar Higher Still

1. 1 Corinthians 2:9-12, *The Holy Bible: New International Version* (NIV).

2. John 14:12-14, Ephesians 2:10, NIV.

3. John 17:23, NIV.

NAME INDEX

227

SUBJECT INDEX

ABOUT THE AUTHOR

HUGH ROSS earned a B.Sc. in physics from the University of British Columbia and an M.Sc. and Ph.D. in astronomy from the University of Toronto. For several years he continued his research on quasars and galaxies as a post-doctoral fellow at the California Institute of Technology. For eleven years he served as minister of evangelism at Sierra Madre Congregational Church.

Today he directs the efforts of Reasons To Believe, an institute founded to research and proclaim the factual basis for faith in God and His Word, the Bible. He also hosts a weekly television program called "Reasons to Believe" on the Trinity Broadcasting Network. Over the years, Dr. Ross has given hundreds of lectures, seminars, and courses, both in the United States and abroad, on Christian apologetics. He is the author of *The Fingerprint of God*, *The Creator and the Cosmos*, and *Creation and Time*. He lives in southern California with his wife, Kathy, and sons, Joel and David.

ABOUT REASONS TO BELIEVE

REASONS TO BELIEVE is a nonprofit organization, without denominational affiliation, adhering to the doctrinal statements of the National Association of Evangelicals and of the International Council on Biblical Inerrancy. It provides research and teaching on the harmony of God's revelation in the words of the Bible and in the facts of nature. Speakers are available for churches, business clubs, university outreaches, etc. A hotline for those with questions or a desire to dialogue on issues pertaining to faith, science, and the Bible operates at (818)335-1480, Monday through Friday, 5-7 P.M., Pacific Time.

A newsletter and a catalog of materials may be obtained by phoning (800)482-7836 or by writing Reasons To Believe, P.O. Box 5978, Pasadena, CA 91117.

The e-mail address is ReasonsTS@aol.com

The Web site is http://www.Reasons.org/Reasons